Scholastic
WORKSHOP

KEY STAGE 1 / SCOTTISH LEVELS A-B

NON-FICTION
Writing Projects

SALLIE HARKNESS,
LYNDA KEITH &
JOYCE LINDSAY

Published by Scholastic Ltd,
Villiers House,
Clarendon Avenue,
Leamington Spa,
Warwickshire CV32 5PR
Text © 1997 Sallie Harkness, Lynda Keith and Joyce Lindsay
© 1997 Scholastic Ltd
3 4 5 6 7 8 9 0   0 1 2 3 4 5 6

Project Consultants
Sue Ellis and Gill Friel

Authors
Sallie Harkness, Lynda Keith and Joyce Lindsay

Editor
Kate Pearce

Assistant Editor
Joel Lane

Series Designer
Joy White

Designer
Anna Oliwa

Illustrations
Ray and Corinne Burrows

Cover illustration
Joy White

Designed using Aldus Pagemaker

British Library Cataloguing-in-Publication Date
A catalogue record for this book
is available from the British Library.

ISBN 0-590-53479-3

Scholastic WORKSHOP

Contents

ACKNOWLEDGEMENTS

The publishers gratefully acknowledge permission to reproduce the following copyright material:

Henderson Publishing plc for the use of text and illustrations from *Start to Draw Animals* © Henderson Publishing plc (1994, Henderson Publishing)

HMSO for the use of text and illustrations from A Highway Code for Young Road Users © Crown Copyright Department of Transport and LARSOA (1996, Department of Transport and LARSOA).

Every effort has been made to trace the copyright holders for the works reproduced in this book and the publishers apologise for any inadvertent omissions.

Scholastic
NON-FICTION WRITING PROJECTS
Workshop

Scholastic WORKSHOP

Chapter One

INTRODUCTION

TEACHING NON-FICTION WRITING

This book provides ten extended writing projects for teachers who want to plan work which meets the non-fiction writing requirements of the National Curricula for England and Wales and for Northern Ireland and the Language Guidelines 5–14 for Scotland. It has been produced in the belief that:

• *Children motivate themselves to write.* When teachers create classroom conditions in which pupils can use ideas and develop skills with others and in play, children write because they need and want to; the writing is fun and satisfying.

• *Teachers should foster children's belief in themselves as writers.* Extended writing projects, in which children live the process from initial ideas to seeing their writing read by others, provide a powerful way to ensure that children feel and act like real writers.

• *Teachers should understand the writing process and what support children require.* Teachers must be familiar with the techniques that writers use and encourage children to use them also. They must plan the sequence, structure and pace of writing projects and provide support by planning the organisation and management of writing activities.

• *Teachers should focus on the process, the writer, as well as the writing product.* Teachers who are sensitive to children's needs as writers are observant and analytical of both writer and writing.

The importance of non-fiction writing

Non-fiction is the type of writing most often used in adult life. It is therefore important that children learn how to read and write it and to recognise its special characteristics.

Most young children's awareness of non-fiction writing begins to develop long before they go to school. They notice environmental print and discuss the function and form of the information signs, notices and instructions they see around them. They are interested in, and keen to explore, non-fiction writing through conversation and play.

The teacher's role is to build on these experiences by providing opportunities which should help children to deepen their understanding and knowledge of the variety of purposes and audiences of different types of non-fiction.

Teachers can do this by creating contexts for learning that provide a genuine purpose for writing, harness children's enthusiasm and encourage them to integrate new knowledge and skills. The projects in this book provide opportunities for learning about writing in an integrated, holistic way. Children will use many of the skills, strategies and techniques that are

central to the writer's craft. By taking part in the projects they will begin to understand that different kinds of writing fulfil different purposes. They begin to realise what the reader needs to know – and how this affects what the writer wants to say. This helps the teacher to plan a broad and balanced curriculum and provides a framework within which children can become aware of what they know and can do.

Work within the projects will indicate that children may also need to engage in targeted activities that focus on particular aspects and specific features of non-fiction writing. You will find such activities in the *Non-fiction Writing Skills (KS1)* book, which complements the writing projects in this book. Some of these activities are linked thematically to the projects which follow.

Non-fiction genres

Genre theory provides a new and different focus for the teaching of non-fiction writing. The primary emphasis is on the *purpose* of a piece of writing, rather than its format. Thus, for example, a letter may recount experiences, give instructions or try to persuade. To become effective writers, young children need to recognise the different purposes of non-fiction writing and – through discussion and explicit teaching – begin to learn the organisational features and language characteristics that each purpose requires.

Genres provide a framework which allow the teacher quickly to identify appropriate vocabulary and organisational features which might form the teaching content for any piece of writing. Different genres involve organising and presenting knowledge in different ways. Teachers need to be familiar with the range of genres and to appreciate how they can serve different learning objectives. This knowledge and understanding will enable them to select and structure appropriate writing tasks to deepen children's learning.

Genre theorists working in Australia and Britain have identified six different types or genres of non-fiction: recount, report, persuade, discuss, explain and procedural. Each genre has its own purpose and set of characteristics.

With young children in mind the genres have been grouped under three main headings.
Instructions and directions: This is essentially *procedural writing*, including orders and rules, as well as instructions, on how to make something, recipes and directions for how to get somewhere. Children do this when they

write directions to tell others how to get to their house; a recipe for how to make a pizza; instructions for how to make a model or use a particular piece of equipment, or, sometimes, rules for games.

Persuasion and discussion: This is writing to persuade others, or to present different viewpoints and reach a conclusion (though the latter often poses problems for young writers). Children do this when they write advertising posters and jingles, or speeches to present a particular argument in a debate.

Information writing: This includes *recounts*, *reports* and *explanations*, as these share certain features.

• Recount – a sequence of events, usually told in the order in which they occurred. This is possibly the closest form of non-fiction writing to a story. When children write about a school trip; newspaper articles or an experiment in science, they often write in this genre.

• Report – provides factual information about a topic. This is the genre adopted in many non-fiction books. The writer identifies a number of key issues and writes clearly and concisely about each. Writing about topics for class and individual projects often takes this form.

• Explanation – explains how and why something happens or works. This type of writing is often combined with report or recount writing. Children are often required to do this in describing such things as how a model works, how ice is formed, why puddles dry up on a sunny day or how a tadpole develops into a frog.

Project	Type	Instructions/ directions	Persuasion/ discussion
Please visit our class	Planning an Open Day for visitors to the classroom	Writing directions for the visitors	Designing posters to persuade the visitors to come
Signs around us	Looking at local environment; gaining information from signs	Reading, planning and making signs to instruct	Reading, planning and making signs to persuade
Our good toy guide	Practical investigation of toys and their good/bad features and suitability	Following instructions to make a book	Justifying choices and recognising other's opinions; reaching conclusions
Weather station	Taking part in a local study which involves observation, investigation and research		Designing a poster linking types of weather with different activities
Dinosaur museum	Setting up a 'small world' museum in the classroom	Writing instructions about how to make or draw a dinosaur	Persuading another class to visit the museum
Memories	History focus; people and places in the past; personal, class and family memories		
Fairy tales revisited	Imaginative context set in Storyland – setting up an Estate Agency		Persuading people to buy houses; justifying reasons in response to a persuasive letter
Time all around	Using children's own experiences of time in and out of school		
Changes	Focus on concept of changes in nature and people; learning and transmitting information	Following instructions to make pages of a book	Advantages and disadvantages of some changes
Me, looking after myself	Children looking at themselves and how they can look after themselves; topic including healthy living	Writing instructions for keeping clean – How to wash your face	Creating a menu for healthy eating; poster about keeping safe

Scholastic
NON-FICTION WRITING PROJECTS
Workshop

Giving information	Collaborative demands	Approximate timescale	Publication format
Using a variety of formats to give information about the class	Low	Two/three weeks	Open day visit for children's family with information posters and displays
Reading, planning and making signs to persuade	High	Two/three weeks	Making signs for class, playroom, school and playground
Giving information in different ways; importance of fact and accuracy; recording information from texts	High	Two/three weeks	Book – Our Good Toy Guide
Survey, observation, chart, weather preferences, letter writing, research and interviews	High	Four weeks	Personal/group folders; classroom display; presentation at school assembly
Creating a variety of information books; designing a survey	Medium	Two weeks	Display of writing generated through the project; Small world dinosaur museum
Reporting on past experiences; recording past experiences; taking notes, making lists, charts	Low	Two/three weeks	Video presentation 'Our journey into the past'
Writing information about the characters and different houses in Storyland	Low	Two weeks	All writing contributing to a Storyland Estate Agency
Giving information by recounting, reporting and sequencing information about time	Medium	Two/three weeks	Display using a variety of writing formats
Reading for information; writing reports, explanations and illustrating pages	High	Three/four weeks	Group encyclopaedia/ information book 'Changes'
About me – taking exercise, resting, sleeping, family and friends; thank you letter; interview questions; book format – cover design, contents page, index	Low	Three/four weeks	Each child creates an individual book which is dedicated to the special person of their choice

NON-FICTION WRITING PROJECTS

This volume contains
• ideas and session plans for ten writing projects that can be done with the whole class, simplifying organisation and planning;
• photocopiable activity sheets linked to each project;
• ideas for publishing, review and celebration of the children's work;
• suggestions, advice and photocopiable pages for assessment and record-keeping.

The importance of extended writing

Each project builds up a particular context over a period of two to four weeks, allowing children to become immersed in it for long enough to become emotionally involved and committed to the suggested writing tasks. Because each session provides a springboard for the next, the children have time to think and plan, develop language skills and extend vocabulary, and discuss and reflect on their work. They can raise questions, take the initiative and be active in their own learning.

Writing for real

When children write for a range of audiences they will take the tasks seriously because they want to see the end results. Feedback sessions, both during and at the end of the projects, help young writers to reassess and understand what

the reader needs to know. It also increases the writers' self-esteem to know that their writing is being read by real readers, whether these are their classmates, other classes, parents, the headteacher or other people outside the school.

The importance of play

Play is one way in which children develop a sense of ownership, assimilate new ideas and open up new possibilities by developing their ideas. Many of the projects use play situations in which the teacher can observe children's interests and understanding, and pick up and develop the ideas they generate.

The projects also use art, drama and role-play activities as valuable ways of exploring and organising ideas.

What do the projects cover?

The ten projects in this book give teachers a range of contexts. They have been selected to reflect the interests and developmental needs of the age-group. Some are generic topics based on children's experience of real-life events. All the projects establish and maintain close links with different aspects of the curriculum.

Because this book is a resource, not a scheme, it offers maximum flexibility if used by all teachers/children working in Years 1–3 or at KS1. In this way individual teachers or the whole staff can ensure progression and coherence across year groups.

The ten projects vary in difficulty and interest levels. Some have been designed with Year 1 pupils in mind, others for Year 2 and Year 3. A series of projects undertaken during the first three years enables teachers to plan for progression in skills and continuity. The chart on pages 8-9 summarises topics, genres and curriculum areas for each project.

Building and reinforcing knowledge of non-fiction genres

Each project involves children writing in a variety of non-fiction genres. Teachers can select projects which will challenge the children by developing and building on previous work, or can carry out a project that introduces less familiar genres to ensure overall balance.

The varied writing activities of the projects provide opportunities to teach aspects of the different genres in use, and to note their special features. By encouraging this kind of discussion the teacher can bring together and reinforce pupils' learning and knowledge of language.

CLASSROOM MANAGEMENT

Whole-class projects simplify teacher planning and resource provision and give the teacher more time to observe, teach and work alongside children.

Involving the whole class in a project motivates children to investigate and discuss, and also to take part in collaborative group work. The teacher can harness their enthusiasm and draw on collective experience and skills. A successful project will reach out into the rest of the school and become part of life at home and even the community as children involve family and friends.

Project sessions have been designed to motivate young writers and to take account of the wide diversity of skills in Years 1–3. As the topic is developed, children should have opportunities to work in pairs or in a group to share ideas and support each other. In this way writing will be a challenging but social activity.

The projects help children to develop a sense of the writing process and of themselves as writers. They also help them to understand more about the nature of the written product and the features which help the reader to understand what the writer is trying to say.

It is important to work through the child's understanding to help him or her to clarify both the message (what he or she wants to say) and what the reader wants to know. In working with children, teachers need to target both the process and the content knowledge that lead to an appropriate product. Some ways you can scaffold children's learning are by:

(1)   Talking with children about their writing. Conferencing with groups and individuals enables the teacher to model being a good writing partner.
• Ask the child about what she or he wants to say.
• Ask the child to evaluate her or his work – what are its strengths and weaknesses?
• Tell the child something you like about what he or she has written and why.
• Send the child away with one thing to think about and change.

(2)   Encouraging children, particularly the youngest ones, to represent and clarify their understanding in a variety of ways, for example talking, drawing and model-making. The teacher's task may be to help the child to create

an oral statement which can be scribed.

(3)   Being explicit about the needs and expectations of the reader and about the features that will help the reader to understand, and being willing to help the child to appreciate these by:
• helping children to select and clarify main ideas and to sequence and express them in a way which is clear and concise;
• building on children's suggestions and ideas;
• modelling formats and drawing attention to features;
• encouraging reflection and evaluation by discussing their work and giving specific praise and encouragement.

Using the projects

Where you start depends on your individual needs and those of your class. You need to be sure that, in the course of the school year, the class have opportunities to write in a range of genres and contexts. Obviously children must experience the required/recommended curriculum in line with national guidelines and school policy. However, it is still possible – and essential – to find starting points which reflect the needs, interests and abilities of the children.

How to start

You may choose a project because it:
• fits with a particular class's interests, or a local or topical issue;
• targets a particular cross-curricular theme or topic;

• targets particular types or genres of writing you want to develop.

When you choose a project, consider the children's previous writing experiences, their level of independence and their ability to work in groups. Some projects involve children in research which requires certain levels of reading ability. Reviewing the project descriptions, teaching points and star ratings will help you to make an informed choice of project.

You should also take into account:
• the writing processes involved;
• the particular genres and frameworks entailed;
• the skills and sub-skills children learn;
• the organisational and resourcing demands.
A flexible plan can then be created which can be further adapted to take account of how children are responding and progressing.

Planning time for projects

Young children need to be involved in the project activities on a daily basis and blocks of time should be reserved for the writing tasks. Approximate timescales for the projects are given on pages 8-9. However, you may choose to lengthen the time allocation if the children's interest grows. If certain subject areas receive less attention for a week or two, plan to redress the balance in future weeks.

Organising the class

Some projects require space for the children's imaginative play or investigative activities. Specific requirements of each project are detailed in the chart on pages 8-9.

If you do not have the space for a permanent play area in your classroom, collect resources for children to play with in a box or play bag which may be given to groups of children at appropriate times.

Display space for artwork and writing is needed so that children can monitor and assess their progress during a project, as well as celebrate and appraise the final results.

You may see advantages in providing continuity of grouping within a topic or it may be advisable to keep groups flexible. Some groups specify group continuity. Clearly there are advantages in friendship grouping. For project work, mixed ability groups may be the best choice.

Choosing and organising resources

Children value their work more if they are given good quality materials. Make paper available in a range of shapes, sizes and colours.

Colouring crayons, pencils, marker pens, adhesive and scissors are also required. Each pupil should have a personal folder in which to keep his or her work. Word-processed printouts give a professional finish to children's work for display or publication.

Publication, celebration and review

Publication and presentation of art and written work is an integral part of each project. It helps to foster a sense of achievement and ownership. A variety of publication formats is offered (see grid on pages 8-9 for full details).

When a project is completed, children may celebrate their work by discussing and evaluating it with each other or by sharing it with others outside the classroom – parents, another class, the headteacher or a special guest. Planning these events gives the project direction and is a satisfying way to end it. If the project is shared with people outside the classroom this provides a new audience for the children's writing. Partnerships between home and school, and between school and community, are developed. Positive feedback from the visitors can encourage children to evaluate the project and the part they all played in it.

Project activities provide opportunities for parents to share interests and experiences with their children and to become aware of their children's learning.

KEY TO SYMBOLS

[*] [**] [***]	level of difficulty of the activity
(35)	approximate duration of the activity in minutes (a blank clock indicates an untimed activity)
≋	photocopiable page for classroom use
†	each child in the group working individually
††	children working in pairs
††††	a small group collaborating
Ⓦ	whole class or larger group working together

Chapter Two,
ASSESSMENT

ASSESSMENT

In the first years at school the approach to assessment should be 'light touch' with an emphasis on celebrating children's achievements in order to enhance positive feelings about themselves as writers. It is also important to discover children's interests and preferences and to begin to keep accurate records of which topics have been covered so as to maintain continuity, ensure progression and avoid repetition. Parents need to be informed of progress as do other teachers who will work with the children.

The process of assessment and record-keeping should support teachers in monitoring children's progress thus enabling them to identify needs and to plan appropriate teaching and learning activities. The non-fiction writing projects enable the teacher to observe children over an extended period of time and to build up an informed view of each child based on evidence from talk, play, drawing and writing. Assessment of non-fiction writing in these project settings will focus on the same genre features listed in the companion volume *Non-fiction Writing Skills (KS1)*.

Teachers will wish to plan their approach to assessment in a way which takes account of their school's assessment policy and requirements. They will also need to ascertain how assessment is being tackled in other aspects of the writing programme. Consideration should be given to the recommendations of the National Curricula for England and Wales and the Language 5-14 Guidelines for Scotland.

General assessment and record-keeping photocopiable pages

Three assessment and record-keeping sheets for teacher use are provided in this book. These can be used alongside the project activities to build up a profile of individual and group development, and to keep a record of group and class work.

Class/group project notes (page 16)

The class/group project notes are intended to provide an informal record of any project. General comments may be noted under the heading 'The project in class'.

The heading 'Non-fiction writing development' has been designed to enable the teacher to identify any children who 'stood out', noting why they attracted attention. If this sheet is used throughout the project, on a daily basis if necessary, it will soon become apparent which children are attracting attention and for what reasons. Consideration can then be given to others: are they performing satisfactorily, or just being overlooked?

The three main genres, 'Instructions/ Directions', 'Persuasion/Discussion' and 'Giving information' are provided to enable further detail to be recorded.

Individual project report (page 17)

The individual project report helps the teacher to analyse each child's work, to identify achievement and to note success. It has also been designed to enable the teacher to suggest where support is required. Three areas are highlighted:

• The child as a non-fiction writer

Space is given to record the child's preferences, which activities were enjoyed, and for the teacher to comment on what the child found easy or difficult.

It also allows the teacher to comment on the child's preferred strategies for planning and writing, awareness of purpose and audience, and the child's attitude, commitment and involvement.

• Teacher comment on the use of genre

This allows the teacher to record how the child tackled the various tasks; to assess and analyse skills level; and to note the child's awareness of the particular features of the different genres.

• Teacher–child discussion

A number of the projects provide an evaluation sheet for the child to complete at the end of the project. This allows the teacher to record and comment on the child's evaluation in the light of the teacher's own observations.

The teacher must decide when to complete an individual project report. It is not essential that a report is done for each child in every project although there should be a plan to assess all the children over a period of time.

Overall class record of projects (page 18)

This is a record of the writing projects covered each year and can be passed on to subsequent teachers of the class.

Providing feedback to the child

Children need to be given advice and encouragement throughout the project, but use of the assessment formats provided will inform the teacher of what advice and support children may require in future.

It is important to appreciate the role of celebration in enabling children to value their work and that done by others. This helps to build self esteem and confidence, creating a favourable attitude to the next piece of work.

Self evaluation and peer evaluation

Self evaluation is important because it increases children's awareness of their knowledge and skills. Some of the projects provide an evaluation sheet. If desired these can be used to model further sheets. Children can use these sheets to

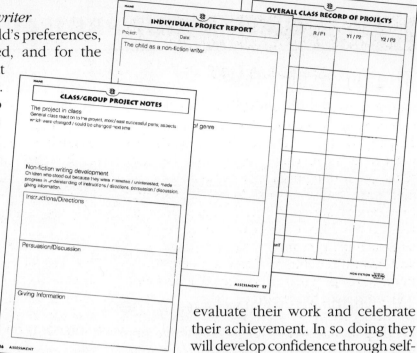

evaluate their work and celebrate their achievement. In so doing they will develop confidence through self-knowledge. This in turn builds self-esteem. Information from this sheet can be used by the teacher to identify learning needs.

Opportunities for peer evaluation have been built in to many of the project sessions. Children can often analyse the work of others better than their own. They have to explain their ideas and justify their opinions. This helps clarify and consolidate their understanding and knowledge of language. They may respond differently to writing created by someone they know rather than more distant professional authors. Discussion of this should contribute to establishing stronger links between reading and writing.

Summative assessment

It is suggested that the teacher builds up a portfolio of work for each child. This is different from the child's folder which is merely a storing place for pieces of work undertaken as part of the project. A selection of writing should be made for the portfolio. This might include first drafts, final copies, comments from the teacher and the child, writing review forms, and so on.

The teacher will decide on how to identify work for the portfolio. Options include:

• teacher selection – adult viewpoint
• child selection – writer's viewpoint
• negotiated selection – child and teacher work together
• key tasks identified in advance as being for the portfolio

Practical considerations, such as storage, ownership and access, and future use, also require to be addressed.

CLASS/GROUP PROJECT NOTES

The project in class
General class reaction to the project, most/least successful parts; aspects which were changed / could be changed next time.

Non-fiction writing development
Children who stood out because they were interested / uninterested; made progress in understanding of instructions / directions, persuasion / discussion, giving information.

Instructions/Directions

Persuasion/Discussion

Giving Information

INDIVIDUAL PROJECT REPORT

Project: Date:

The child as a non-fiction writer

Teacher comment on the use of genre

Teacher-child discussion

OVERALL CLASS RECORD OF PROJECTS

Projects	R / P1	Y1 / P2	Y2 / P3
Please visit our class			
Signs around us			
Our good toy guide			
Weather station			
Dinosaur museum			
Memories			
Fairy tales revisited			
Time all around			
Changes			
Me, looking after myself			

Scholastic
WORKSHOP

Chapter Three

PLEASE VISIT OUR CLASS

INTRODUCTION

Project description

This project involves the children in planning, organising and carrying through arrangements for a Class Open Day for family and/or friends. Children first of all identify the types of information that they will need to know to plan the visit, and then create a list of tasks to carry out.

The children participate in a sequence of activities arising from this list, starting with the design of individual posters identifying good reasons to visit their class. Using a simple questionnaire, children gather information about visitors, design a 'Welcome' poster, write directions to the class and create a programme for the Open Day. On the day, children entertain the guests. Afterwards both children and guests evaluate the success of the Open Day.

Why this context?

Children enjoy having visitors and this project encourages children to take pride in their own classroom. It also helps to foster home/school links.

The project has a variety of opportunities for functional writing and contains activities which will develop the children's ability to communicate information using a variety of publishing formats. These include invitations, posters, questionnaires, biographies, leaflets, recipes and programmes.

Project organisation

The activities in this project involve a balance of whole class, group and individual tasks. All the children contribute towards planning the Open Day. The project may last two or three weeks or it may be part of a larger project about 'Our School'. Some preparatory planning in arranging the date will be necessary and you may require additional support from teachers or parents on the day itself. Involvement with the children's families will also be required in order to clarify details needed to organise the Open Day.

Publication, celebration and review

All of the materials created by the children in preparation for the Open Day can be displayed in the classroom – photographs which they will have taken, information posters and biographies. Other class work can be labelled and displayed on a project table for the visitors to read. You may also like to provide a visitors' book for people to sign.

Finally evaluation sheets are used to provide a review of what visitors and children liked and enjoyed finding out about during the Open Day.

Books the children may find useful

Look Around The School, Clive Pace and Jean Birch (1992) Wayland
The Class Teacher, Diana Bentley (1987) Wayland

Gather the children together and tell them that they are going to invite family or friends to visit their classroom. Explain that this will involve a lot of planning – they must think about:

- who to invite;
- how to invite them;
- what needs to be done in the classroom;
- what to do on the day.

Ask the children to think about these for the next day and come back with some ideas.

1

PLEASE VISIT OUR CLASS BECAUSE...

Teaching content
Lists can consist of a few words and may be prioritised. To persuade someone to come to visit the class we have to think of a relevant reason.

What you need
Large sheets of paper, marker pens, photocopiable page 29, writing and drawing materials.

What to do
Bring the class together and remind the children that they have to make plans for the visit. Using a large sheet of paper, make a list of the children's suggestions of 'Things to do'. These may include:

- making a poster;
- sending invitations;
- deciding when the visit will happen;
- making the room look interesting.

There may be too many items on the list for the children to carry out, but assure them that they will all be very involved because it is their class. Tell the children that they need to sort the items on the list into things that need to be done soon, things that need to be done later and on-going activities that need to be carried out in preparation for the day. Ask the children, 'What shall we do first? What shall we do later?'

Suggest to the children that perhaps the first thing to do is to inform their family that this event will be happening soon and tell them why they should visit this class.

Ask the children why they think that this is a good class to visit. How will they persuade parents and friends to come? What is special about their class? They may have varied reasons such as:

- it's a happy place;
- we work hard here;
- there is lots to do;
- you can meet the children;
- you can see what we do.

Again, scribe their suggestions on a large sheet of paper so that the children can copy whichever they like.

Give each child a copy of photocopiable page 29 and tell them these will be their invitations to take home. Ask them to choose one of the reasons that has been given, or another of their choice, and complete the sentence at the top of the sheet. (Depending on the age and ability of the children, you may have to scribe or supply words.) The children should then draw a picture in the box underneath their writing to illustrate what they have written. Children can decorate the border personally, drawing objects in the classroom or children's faces. Ask the children to write their name in the box at the bottom of the sheet. Keep the partially completed sheets for use in the next session.

At the end of this session, ask the children to think about what other information about the Open Day they need to put on their invitations.

Things to do

WHAT DO WE NEED TO KNOW?

W → ✝ → W 60

Teaching content

In writing invitations we have to be clear about the information we need and how we will collect it.

What you need

Variety of invitation cards, large sheet of paper, marker pens, children's partially completed copies of photocopiable page 29, photocopiable page 30, pre-prepared invitation cards (one for each child, approx. 11cm by 6cm, with 'Please come to', 'on', 'at' written on them), writing materials, adhesive.

What to do

At the beginning of this session gather the children together and tell them the date for the Open Day. Give them back the invitations on photocopiable page 29 that they partially completed in the previous session. Explain that now the date is fixed they will be able to add this to their invitations. Ask them what other information they should write on the invitations. Show the children the selection of invitation cards which you have brought in. What is on all of these? The children will probably point out the date, time, where to come and the request for a reply. (If you feel it is appropriate at this stage you may like to explain the term R.S.V.P.)

List their responses on a large sheet of paper. Decide with the children the most appropriate time for the visit and what they should write for the location of the class. At this point 'Class 2' or 'Room 3' may be sufficient. Write this in large print for children to see or copy on to their own invitations.

Give each child a pre-prepared invitation card and ask them to fill in the information about where and when to come and the time of the visit. Tell the children to stick this in the box at the foot of their invitation sheets. Now the children have completed the invitation to take home.

Bring the children back together and explain that to prepare for the Open Day they need to find out a few things in advance. Show them a copy of photocopiable page 30 and discuss the sheet with them, explaining that they will need to take this sheet home. Tell them that when they are completed, the sheets will provide information about:

• how many people will be coming;
• what they would like to eat;
• the visitors' familiarity with the location of the classroom;
• what they would like to find out about.

This involvement will hopefully make children feel part of the organisation of the event and provide an opportunity for them to see adults filling in a simple questionnaire. Give a reply date for the return of the questionnaire to enable planning of future sessions. Send this home along with the child's personal invitation.

3

GATHERING THE INFORMATION

⚙/ 👥 ⏱ 50

Teaching content

Information sometimes needs to be ordered according to importance or priority. It can be collated in a numbered list.

What you need

Completed photocopiable page 30, five large sheets of paper (labelled: no. of people (1, 2); chocolate cake, biscuit; know, need directions; find out about; things to do) marker pens, scissors, adhesive.

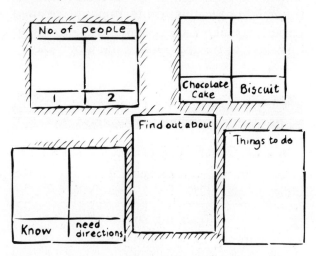

What to do

Note: The timing of this session will be dependent on the children bringing back their completed copies of photocopiable page 30 from home. (If you have a large class, this may be more effectively managed one group at a time, while the rest of the children are engaged on other tasks.)

Begin by asking the children to cut out the seven information boxes on photocopiable page 30, and carefully bring these pieces of paper to the gathering area.

Explain to the children that they have lots of different pieces of information and that, for it to make sense and to help in the planning, it is useful to gather all of the information together. Begin with the information about the number of visitors. Explain that the children should stick the box which has been ticked at home on to the appropriate sheet of paper. So, for example, if 'Two people will come' has been ticked, the child will attach it to the sheet with

that heading. Repeat with the other boxes about food and directions.

Continue to collate the information until all the children have attached their boxes to the large sheets. Gather the children together and count:
• how many visitors will probably come;
• how many chocolate cakes/biscuits will have to be made;
• how many leaflets will be needed giving directions to the classroom.
(Some parents may give answers which do not match the headings on the photocopiable sheet. If this happens you will need to list these separately, for example if a parent has written 'could vary' under the number of people who will be coming.)

Finally read what has been written in the 'On the visit I/we would like to find out about...' box with the children and list the areas of interest in the classroom.

Now decide on a list of 'things to do' with the children. Review the list generated in Session 1 and, using the information gathered in this session, make a fresh list of the activities that need to be carried out. Write these on the fifth large sheet of paper, so that it can be kept on display for the children to see. Talk with them about which activities need to be done first, next and last, and sequence these in order of priority.

For the next session, ask the children to think about five interesting things they could write about themselves and their classroom which can be included on welcome posters for the visitors.

WELCOME TO OUR CLASS (1)

Teaching content

In writing information about yourself, you have to consider what the audience will find relevant and interesting.

What you need

Large sheet of paper, marker pens, photocopiable page 31, writing and drawing materials, coloured paper.

What to do

Begin by gathering the children together and discussing their thoughts about welcome posters for the classroom. Ask the children 'Why should we make a poster? What does a poster tell us? What may be on it?'

Tell the children that they will all have an opportunity to draw a picture of themselves and write their name, but that you also want them to write five interesting things about themselves and their classroom, for instance what they like, what they do in the classroom, what areas may be of interest to the visitors, and so on. Spend some time on this, taking suggestions and encouraging children to think

of who will be reading these points.

On a large sheet of paper, write down some of the children's suggestions so that they can be shared by the whole class. For example:

- I like to go to PE on Monday.
- I like reading books in the book corner.
- We have an interest table with books about dinosaurs.
- I help with the paints.
- Sometimes I take notes to the school office.

Distribute a copy of photocopiable page 31 to each child and discuss the sheet with the class. Ask the children to fill in their name, draw a small picture of themselves in the box and then write their five interesting points. (You may prefer to work with one group at a time, depending on how much support is needed in scribing or providing words.)

When completed, mount the sheets (or let the children do this) on to brightly coloured paper, or make a frieze entitled 'Welcome to our class' to be displayed at the Open Day.

WELCOME TO OUR CLASS (2)

Teaching content

In creating an information poster we need to think about a title, the layout and the relevance of the information.

What you need

A4 paper, card or coloured paper (large enough to display four A4 pictures and a heading), writing and drawing materials.

What to do

Praise the children for the work undertaken in creating the display from the previous session. Tell them that they are now going to make an information poster for each area of the room so that the visitors know what happens there. The content of these posters will depend on the areas within your classroom but may include a

- book corner;
- display table;
- art/craft area;
- home corner;
- construction area.

Put the children into groups of four and allocate one area to each group. Ask them to go to their particular area for a few minutes to think about the kinds of activities they do there, what a visitor might want to know about it and what they could write about or draw for the visitors. At the end of this time, gather the children together again and listen to their suggestions. For example, one group might say, 'In the book corner we read lots of books, listen to stories, sit together and look at pictures.'

Still working in their groups, hand out one sheet of A4 paper to each child and ask them to begin by drawing a picture of their allocated area. Try to encourage a variety of pictures to

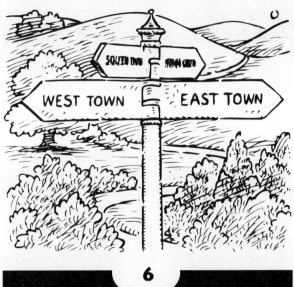

Figure 1

convey the information, but this is less important than all the children being able to contribute to a poster. When they have finished, combine each child's drawings into one large poster per group. Depending on the children's ability to scribe, labels may be added under the drawings or around the poster. Encourage the children to make the labels as this is important in developing their understanding and awareness of layout. Figure 1 shows an example of how the finished poster may look.

Finally, make time for the groups to tell each other about their posters and encourage the children to ask questions of each other. Explain to the children that you will display the posters in their appropriate areas for the visitors to look at. Children may be allocated to answer questions about 'their' area as part of the day.

CAN YOU FIND YOUR WAY HERE?

Teaching content
Directions need to be written simply and clearly. They usually begin with an action word and use particular vocabulary to show sequence. For example, 'go', 'turn', 'pass', 'first', 'next', 'then'. Arrows and signs can also help.

What you need
Photocopiable page 32 (plus an enlarged copy for demonstration with the class), examples of different directions and signs, writing and drawing materials.

What to do
Although desirable, it may not be possible to undertake this activity with the whole class. Since it involves children thinking about writing directions from the entrance of the school to the classroom, it will involve movement around the school. How you arrange this session will depend largely on your own organisation.

Begin by reminding the children that some visitors had asked for directions to get from the school entrance to the classroom. Since you do not want them to get lost, the children will have to make up a directions sheet and then ask somebody to try it out to check that the directions are simple and correct. The simplicity of the directions will also depend on the location of your classroom. Read and show the children some of the examples which you have found of 'How to get there', emphasising the action words used to give directions, for instance 'go', 'forward', 'pass', 'turn', and so on.

Take the group of children to the entrance of the school and let them talk through giving directions to get to the classroom. Emphasise that directions must be very accurate because if people do not know where to go they will look for signs and symbols to give them directions. As the children talk through each stage of this process, write down the directions they give you. If necessary, stop and ask them questions, and clarify directions in order to be more precise.

On your return to the classroom, review the directions given and show the children the direction frame on your enlarged copy of photocopiable page 32. Sort the directions into four steps – 'first', 'next', 'then', 'finally'. Use words, symbols or a combination of both to show a logical sequence. Leave this enlarged sheet out for the groups to refer to.

Give each child a copy of photocopiable page 32. Encourage the children to work in pairs and to write their own text and devise symbols for a series of directions from the school entrance to their classroom. They may decorate the border with some of the signs seen 'en route' or decorate it with arrows. Let children evaluate the success of their work by allowing other children, perhaps from a different class, to 'walk through' the directions to assess their accuracy. Finally, make sufficient copies of the sheets to send out to the visitors.

Note: If it proves difficult to organise the session in the above way, you may prefer to use a simple floor plan of the school, with children drawing a line from the entrance to the classroom to indicate the route.

LOOK FOR SIGNS AROUND OUR SCHOOL

Teaching content
Signs give information using pictures and words.

What you need
Loaded camera, pre-cut card for mounting photographs and pre-cut paper for writing the accompanying labels, an enlarged copy of photocopiable page 33 for demonstration with the class, writing materials.

What to do
Begin by asking the children what signs they can think of that are in and around the school, for example school name, labels on doors, fire instructions, and so on. Show the children photocopiable page 33 and discuss and compare some of the signs on it. Tell the children that they are going to take photographs of some of the different signs around the school to explain to the visitors on the Open Day. Depending on age, the children may take the photographs (although you may wish to take a back-up set just in case!).

Select a group of children to accompany you round the school to photograph signs which convey information. (There may be implications for the organisation of the rest of the class or the timing of this activity.)

The next part of the session should take place when the photographs have been developed. Begin by recalling where the signs are and what information they give. Depending

on the number of photographs taken, allocate one or two per pair and ask the children to think about what information they would write on a label to tell visitors about the photograph. For example, 'This is the headteacher's room', or 'No smoking or dogs allowed in our school'.

Finally, mount the photographs and the children's labels and display them within the classroom or in the corridor area for the visitors to see. Alternatively, if there is a lack of space, the photographs can be kept in an album with an appropriately titled cover.

8

WELCOME FOOD

Teaching content

Recipes have a title and tell you what you need and what you have to do. They are written as a sequence of instructions. Diagrams and pictures help to make the meaning clear.

What you need

Photocopiable page 34, ingredients, writing and drawing materials, various colours of icing (ready made), A4 paper, chalkboard.

What to do

Refer back to Session 3 and the reviewed 'Things to do' list. Remind the children that they collated information about the number of chocolate cakes and biscuits that would be needed for the visitors. Tell the children that each group will be given a turn to make some of these so that they have enough for the Open Day. Explain to the children that the chocolate cakes and biscuits need to be made as close as possible to the Open Day to ensure that they are still fresh.

Select the first group and organise them in an area suitable for baking. Within the group, select two children to draw or write a recipe instruction at each stage of the process. Give them a sheet of A4 paper.

Show the children the recipes on photocopiable page 34 and explain that these tell them how to make the biscuits and cakes. Show them the titles which tell them what to make and the list of what is needed, and ask the children to check they have all the ingredients. As this is being done, ask the two recipe writers

to write the title at the top of their sheet of paper and draw all of the ingredients, labelling each one and adding the details of amounts where necessary.

Follow the recipe and at each stage tell the 'writers' to record the instructions in pictures and/or words. Draw the children's attention to the accuracy needed in the sequence, and stress that each instruction must begin with an action word.

While the biscuits or cakes are cooking discuss with the children how they will decorate them. They may suggest making a happy face or writing a 'W' for Welcome using icing. Explain that while they are waiting for the cakes or biscuits to cook, you would like each child to write out instructions for the visitors about how to decorate them.

Hand each child an A4 sheet of paper and ask them first of all to complete the title 'How to...'. Underneath they should draw a rectangular box. Inside this they should write or draw the ingredients that are needed. Finally ask them to

draw a larger box underneath the ingredients. Inside this they should write clear, sequential instructions which explain how to decorate the cakes and biscuits. You may like to draw the layout of the sheet on the board for children to refer to.

When the biscuits and cakes have cooled, allow the children to follow their instructions for decorating them. Evaluate with them how clear these are for someone else to follow.

Store the cakes in a suitable place and leave some time for the children to complete their instruction sheets and decorate the borders if they wish. These can be put on display on the day of the visit along with the recipe cards made by the pairs of children.

9

A PROGRAMME OF EVENTS

W → ⁱⁱ 45

Teaching content

A programme of events has to follow a chronological sequence. It gives information about what will happen and who is involved.

What you need

Chalkboard, coloured or plain A4 sheets of paper or card, writing and drawing materials.

What to do

Gather the children together and review arrangements for the 'big day'. Review the 'Things to do' list made in Session 3 and ask the children, 'What has been done?' Remind them that they now know the date, time and number of people, what the visitors would like to find out about and what they would like to eat. They have made individual 'Welcome' posters for the classroom, posters explaining the various areas in the classroom and sheets giving directions to the classroom, taken photographs of signs around the school and made 'Welcome' food for the visitors. Their final task is to prepare a programme of events for the visitors and to decide who will be involved in presenting specific areas.

Talk through the sequence of the visit with the children. This may take the form of:

9.30 Welcome to our class

Things to do and see

9.45 Walk about

10.15 Welcome food

10.30 Thank you

Once you have decided on the sequence of events for the visit, tell the children to work in pairs. Give each pair a sheet of A4 paper or card

and tell them to write the heading 'Welcome to our class. Programme of events' at the top of the sheet. You may need to write this on the board for the children to copy. Remind them of the essential features of the day and the sequence of events and ask them to create a programme that can be given to guests when they arrive for the Open Day. Model this if necessary. The children can illustrate their sheets when they have finished.

10

CELEBRATION AND REVIEW

W → ⁱ 40

Teaching content

Evaluating the Open Day with the children. Identifying modifications they would make if undertaking this project again.

What you need

Photocopiable pages 35 and 36, writing materials.

What to do

As the visitors leave, thank them for their interest in attending the class Open Day and ask them to please fill in photocopiable page 35, indicating :
- what they liked;
- what they enjoyed finding out about;
- any comments.

Explain that this is important in valuing the children's work and that you will discuss these with the children when they have been returned. The responses can then be collated for the children to enjoy again at a later date.

Discuss with the children what they liked best.
- Which was the best activity? Did they prefer the preparation or the event?
- What did they not like? Why was this not popular?
- What would they do for another visit? What would they organise differently? Would there be other things to do?

Using photocopiable page 36, let the children write or draw how they felt about the visit. When this has been completed, provide time for the children to give their responses orally to the whole class. Collate the responses in a class book entitled 'The Visit to Our Class'.

OPEN DAY

Please visit our class because...

name

PLEASE VISIT OUR CLASS

Name: _____

We would like to invite you to visit our class on _____

Would you please fill in this information sheet with your child to help us to plan our Class Open Day. Please tick the appropriate boxes.

Thank you.

One person will come.	Two people will come.
I/We would like to eat a chocolate cake.	I/We would like to eat a biscuit.
I/We know how to get to the classroom.	I/We would like directions to the classroom.

On the visit I/We would like to find out about...
(Please comment)

SOME INTERESTING THINGS

My name is _____

Here are five interesting things about me and my class.

_____

_____

_____

_____

_____

DIRECTIONS TO OUR CLASS

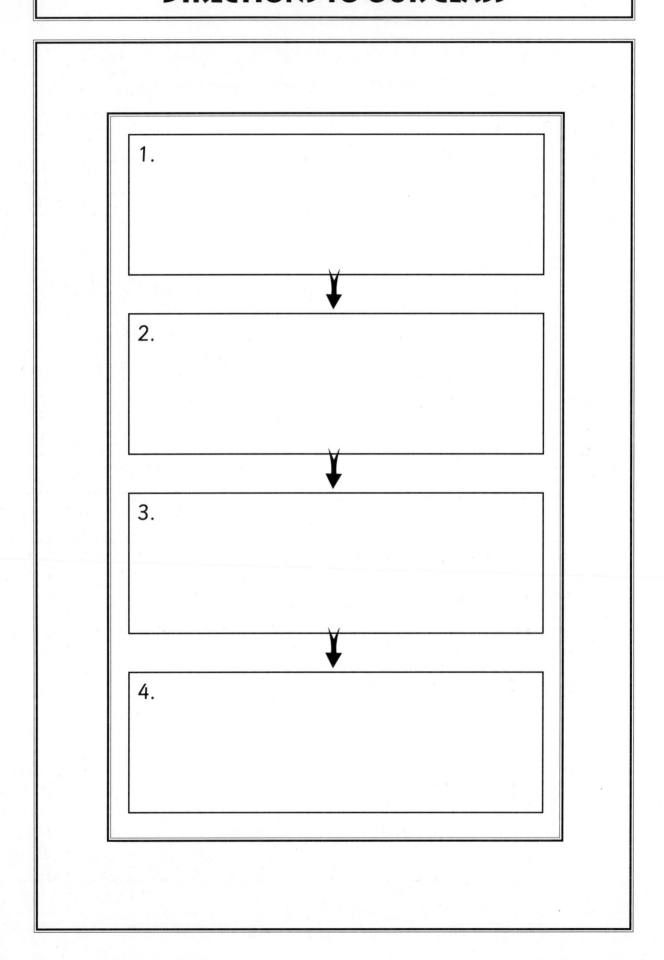

1.

2.

3.

4.

NOTICES AND SIGNS

RECIPES

Biscuits

Ingredients:

150g butter or margarine

75g caster sugar

150g plain flour

50g cornflour

Method

1. Cream butter and sugar using a wooden spoon.

2. Add flour – mix with a spoon and knead.

3. Roll out on a floured board.

4. Cut with a fluted cutter.

5. Prick lightly with a fork.

6. Bake in the oven for 40 minutes at 160°C (Gas Mark 3).

Chocolate cakes (makes 8–10)

Ingredients:

75g flour

75g butter

75g caster sugar

2 eggs (separated)

50g chocolate

1 tablespoon water

Time: 20 minutes

Oven temperature: 180°C

(Gas mark 4)

Method:

1. Cream butter and sugar, add egg yolks and flour.

2. Dissolve chocolate in water, cool, add to mixture.

3. Beat whites until stiff, fold lightly into mixture.

4. Three-quarter fill greased biscuit tins. Bake until well risen and firm to the touch.

CELEBRATION AND REVIEW

On my visit to your class:

I liked

I enjoyed finding out about

Comments

REVIEWING OUR OPEN DAY

I liked

I didn't like

Next time we should

Scholastic
NON-FICTION WRITING PROJECTS
Workshop

Scholastic
WORKSHOP

Chapter Four

SIGNS
AROUND US

INTRODUCTION

Project description

The starting point for this project is the local environment in which the children live. The children make a collection of signs, notices and posters which they see around them. They then analyse these and decide on their key features. Emphasis is placed on what the signs tell them, what makes them effective and clear, the purposes of the signs, the variety of ways in which they are presented and the similarities and differences they see. This leads to children identifying what signs would be useful in the class, playroom, school and playground. They then design, make and test the effectiveness of them.

Why this context?

Young children are naturally curious and notice signs around them. This context provides an ideal opportunity to tune into children's natural curiosity, to develop their observation skills and to introduce them to the variety of functional writing and genres which they see daily and which are beginning to make sense to them. The context is therefore embedded in their own experiences.

By observing, closely sharing and analysing observations, and creating their own examples based on observations, children gain a deeper understanding of the purposes and types of functional print in the world around them.

Project organisation

Class, pair, group and individual opportunities are presented. All children are involved throughout the project and contribute to the wall display and the signs and notices created. It is vital that the children are also involved in a visit to the local environment, either as a class or preferably in smaller groups to collect samples of signs, notices and posters by noting, sketching or photographing what they see. These examples are then used in later activities. Photographs can be especially useful as they provide a resource bank for future work.

As with many areas of work, children will need different amounts and different kinds of help and support at different stages and with different tasks. The activities suggested try to build in this support though only the teacher can judge their suitability and adaptability to her/his pupils.

The duration of the project will vary depending on what is found in the local area and the level of sustainability of children's interest. Two to three weeks as a free-standing project would be reasonable.

Publication, celebration and review

In working through the project a wall display of 'Signs in Our Area' is produced with signs categorised according to their purpose. The main publication is the production of a variety of signs for use in the classroom, playroom, school and playground. Their effectiveness is tested on older children, staff and visitors by posing problems to be solved with reference to the signs.

Books the children may find useful

I-Spy on the Motorway, I-Spy (1996)
I-Spy on a Car Journey, I-Spy (1996)
The Highway Code, HMSO (1996)
Town and Countryside, Barbara Taylor (1995) Black

WE CAN READ AND UNDERSTAND SIGNS

W/ ††††† (45)

Teaching content

There are lots of signs around us which send messages to us. Messages can be sent in different ways depending on the purpose, audience and location. We can try to classify the various signs we see by their purpose.

What you need

An enlarged copy of photocopiable page 48 for demonstration with the class, long strips of paper, chalkboard, writing materials.

What to do

Bring the class together and focus their attention on photocopiable page 48. Ask the children if they recognise any of the signs or symbols.

Take the children's answers in turn and ask questions to deepen their understanding. For example, if a child says she recognises the 'P' sign ask, 'Where have you seen it before? Do you know what it means? Who would be interested in looking at this sign? Why? When? How would it help someone?'

Reinforcement of the children's responses should help to establish that:

• We already know and can read lots of signs.
• Signs send messages.

• Signs are placed and designed for people to read.
• Signs can be helpful.

These key points can be summarised on the board if the children would find this useful. Move on to considering whether all signs are the same or different and why this might be. Ask the children if there are any signs on the sheet which look similar.

Children may identify traffic signs as having red circles or triangles around them but limited written information, such as 10 or STOP. They may also know that many signs use pictures to send messages, for example toilet signs.

The key features to draw out here are that:
• Signs are simple and clear.
• Messages can be given in pictures.
• Messages can be given in writing.
• The writing is often short, direct and large.

Having established these features, the purpose of signs should be reinforced and signs can begin to be classified by intention. This can be done as a class or in groups.

Select one sign from the poster, for example 'Bus Stop'. Explore with the children the purpose of this sign. 'Why do we need a sign for a Bus Stop? What does it tell us?'

Establish that some signs tell us things or impart information. So a first category for the purpose of signs is:

To tell someone something or to give information (category 1).

Write this on a long strip of paper.

Model the process again with another sign, for example 'Wet Paint', and ask the children

why we need a sign that says this. The children will probably identify that this also tells people something. Explore this sign further by asking why people need to know this. Try to establish that this sign is also a warning to people not to touch or they will get paint on their hands or clothes. So another category for the purpose of signs is identified:

To tell people to be careful – to warn people (category 2).
Write this on a long strip of paper.

Other signs can be looked at in the same way, either as a whole class or by allocating different signs to groups for them to suggest categories.

If the children are working in groups, ask them to write their categories on the long strips of paper. These will be used in the next session. Some children may need help deciding on the wording of their categories. In addition to the two categories already noted, ensure that the following categories are identified.
• Signs tell people to do something (category 3);
• Signs tell people rules (category 4);
• Signs tell or persuade people to buy something (category 5).

Appropriate categories are the five given above. To complete the session ask the children to look for one sign on their way home and to sketch it or copy it. Tell them that in the next session the class will be making a collection of the signs they bring in.

SORTING OUR COLLECTION OF SIGNS

Teaching content
Signs have a purpose. We can classify signs as to their purpose.

What you need
Children's notes or sketches of signs, the five categories written on long strips of paper from the previous session, photocopiable page 49, selection of magazines and books (such as *I Spy* books, *Highway Code*), which have a variety of signs, Blu-Tack, A2 sheets, scissors (optional), writing and drawing materials.

What to do
Bring the class together and remind them of the work they did in the previous session. Recall that:
• signs have different purposes;
• these purposes can be classified/categorised.
Refresh the children's memories by looking at one of the signs again, for example 'Bus Stop', and asking them about the purpose of that particular sign.

Look at the categories from Session 1. Remind the children that you asked them to look for one sign on their way home. Take one or two examples from the children and work through the same process as before. 'Why do we have a sign like this? What does it tell us? Which heading or category could we put it under?'

Place the child's note or sketch under the appropriate category. However, explain that some signs may have two purposes. For example, if a child has sketched the symbol in Figure 1 this gives people information and warns them to be careful.

Figure 1

Scholastic
NON-FICTION WRITING PROJECTS
Workshop

Model this with two or three of the children's examples and explain that they may need two sketches – one for each category.

Organise the children into groups and give each group a copy of photocopiable page 49, a sheet of A2 paper and some Blu-Tack. Explain to the children that they are going to work in groups to sort out the signs they have sketched or noted. Two members of the group should arrange the headings from the photocopiable sheet on to the sheet of A2 paper. (If this seems inappropriate you may prefer to prepare the sheets with the headings for each group in advance.) The children must decide what their signs tell people and then, using Blu-Tack, place each one under the appropriate heading. Children can also copy signs from the selection of books you have gathered.

Depending on the children's experience of group work you may like to do this task with one group at a time or allocate specific tasks to children in the group.

At the end each group will have a sheet with signs listed under their appropriate categories. They will find that some signs belong in more than one category and they should be encouraged to find a way of showing this, for example by copying signs (this can be done either by hand or under supervision at the photocopier) or by arranging the categories in a different way, such as using a Venn diagram.

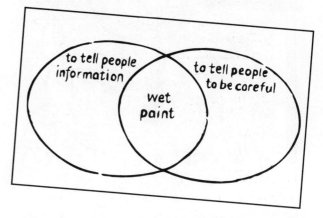

Bring the class together at the end of the session to share their work and explain it to the other groups.

Display these sheets under the caption 'Signs have different purposes. We sorted our signs out.'

draw their group's attention to signs and 'collect' as many different signs as they can. When they find a sign, the children must decide how best to 'collect' it. This could be done by:

- photographing it;
- sketching or drawing it;
- tracing it;
- taking rubbings;
- noting down details.

Set the rules of safety and acceptable behaviour before going out, emphasising possible dangers, for example busy roads. Make sure the children understand that they must never remove, mark or alter a public sign.

Aim for approximately eight to ten signs per group in half an hour. The children can complete their sketches, drawings, and so on, when they return to school. Encourage the groups to recall:

- where they saw each sign;
- what message each sign sends;
- who the message is designed for.

The children can then place their drawings of the signs under the five categories displayed on the group sheets from the previous session.

If photographs were taken, discuss these with the children when they have been developed and decide on their appropriate categories. You may like to provide a set of local photographs for them to make a start on.

3

A SIGN SEARCH
††††† (60)

Teaching content

There are signs in our own area. They are in different places, are meant for different people to read, send different messages and have different ways of sending messages. We can read and understand these signs.

What you need

Loaded camera, clipboards, pencils, sketching paper, tracing paper, crayons, set of local photographs (optional), posters displaying different signs from the previous session.

What to do

The purpose of this session is for the children to note down the range of signs which are in the local area around their school. Ideally it would be best if children could go out in groups of about eight, accompanied by two adults.

Explain to the children that the purpose of their outing is a 'sign search'. They are going to

4

DO WE NEED SIGNS?
††††† (60)

Teaching content

Investigating if and where we may need signs; noting what these might be; planning to make appropriate signs.

What you need

Clipboards, writing materials, photocopiable page 50.

What to do

Note: The content of this session can be covered in two ways depending on the availability of other adults to supervise groups of children. If a sufficient number of adults or senior pupils are available to work with groups of six children the whole class can work on this at the same time. If this is not possible then one group with an adult can work on it each day during worktime or choosing time.

Bring the class together and remind them of the work they have already carried out on signs and their purposes. Ask the children whether they think some more signs may be needed in the school. Pose some questions. For instance: 'If I was a visitor would I know how to get to the school office? We know not to run in the corridor but is there a sign telling everyone this rule?'

Ask the children for other suggestions. Explain that they are going to design some signs for the school for use by the school community but first they must decide what signs are needed and where they should be placed.

With the children brainstorm a list of places in the school which may require signs. For example:
• the playground;
• the school entrance;
• the corridors;
• the dining hall;
• the gym hall;
• the playroom;
• the toilets.

Allocate one area to each group. Give each group clipboards, writing materials and several copies of photocopiable page 50. Look at the photocopiable sheet with the children and explain that their task initially is to visit the area with their helper and to identify what signs are needed. They should note these down and where they should be placed on their photocopiable sheet. Their list should include warning signs, information signs and signs which give orders or try to persuade people to do something. A list of possibilities is provided in the column opposite.

POSSIBLE SIGNS
Playground
Don't drop litter – Put it in the bin.
Play together.
Never bully others.
What to do in an accident.
Never leave the playground without permission.
Line up at the bell.
Timetable for the football pitch.
Report broken glass.

Entrance, Corridors
Welcome, Entrance, Exit.
This way to the office.
First Aid is here.
Tuck Shop/Times/Price List.
Caretaker's room.
Room numbers, teachers' names.
Fire Drill.
Please walk in the corridor.
Lost Property.
Toilets.

Dining Hall
Please queue here.
Menu and Price List.
Please pay here.
Remember to clear up your dishes!
Packed Lunches.
Don't waste food.

Playroom/Classroom
Work quietly in the book corner.
Four people can play in the house.
Work together on the computer.
Remember to tidy your desk!
Finished work goes here.
Timetable of the week.
Rules for the sand area.

On returning to the class the helper should make sure that the ideas the children have noted down are clear and that the children understand them as they will be using them in the next session.

The next three sessions – Sessions 5, 6 and 7 – give the children the opportunity to create the signs which they have identified as being necessary on photocopiable page 50.

The format of each session is the same:
1. Identify signs which have the same purpose, for example to tell people to be careful.
2. Identify the key features of signs which share this purpose.
3. Select a sign to design.
4. Plan and design that sign.
5. Evaluate the sign with the group using photocopiable page 51.
6. Create a final copy of the sign.

The signs created will be displayed in the place recognised as needing that sign. The effectiveness of the sign will be tested.

MAKING OUR SIGNS: WARNINGS

Teaching content

Designing signs which are clear, concise and can be understood. Testing these on our friends. Key features of warning signs.

What you need

Completed photocopiable page 50 from the previous session, photocopiable page 51,

Figure 2

photocopiable page 48 (optional), green highlighter pens, scrap paper, card, writing and drawing materials, chalkboard.

What to do

Explain to the class that each group has investigated what signs are needed, why they are needed and where they are needed. Choose one of the children's examples to illustrate this. For instance, if one group went to the playground they may have decided that a notice was required which said 'Don't touch broken glass'. Ask the children, 'What kind of sign is this? What is its purpose?' With the children reach the conclusion that it gives us a warning.

Ask each group to identify any signs on their list which are warning signs. Tell them to highlight these warning signs in green.

Explain to the children that they are going to design signs for the examples they have highlighted, but first you are going to remind them of the key features of warning signs. Select an example either from the wall collection or from photocopiable page 48. Figure 2 gives an example.

Identify that:
- the red triangle indicates a warning;
- the picture is clear and indicates potential danger;
- the writing is clear and tells you what to do or what to be careful of;
- the sign is not overloaded and is very direct.

Ensure that the children understand these key features before setting them the task of designing their own warning signs.

Each group should share the warning signs among the group and decide which one they would like to work on and whether they wish to work alone or with a partner. If they do not have enough they could work on the same signs and compare ideas later.

First attempts should be made in draft form on scrap paper. When these are complete, give each child a copy of photocopiable page 51. Each sign should be evaluated by the rest of the group using the questions on the photocopiable sheet. The designer of the sign should then redraft as necessary, using the advice offered by their group to create a final version of the sign.

Store these sheets when the children have finished referring to them as they will be used to assess the children's signs in the next two sessions.

When the signs are completed they should be taken to their location and pinned up by the children where and how they feel is appropriate.

MAKING OUR SIGNS: ORDERING AND PERSUADING

Teaching content

Designing signs which are clear, concise and can be understood. Testing these on our friends. Key features of signs which persuade or give orders.

What you need

Photocopiable pages 50, 51 and 48 (from the previous session), orange highlighter pens, scrap paper, card, writing and drawing materials, chalkboard.

What to do

This session takes the same form as the previous session, except that this time the children identify and highlight in orange signs which tell people to do something or buy something. They are looking at signs which order or persuade.

Model some examples to clarify the key features for the children. For example, if you use a sign such as that in Figure 3

Figure 3

identify that:
- the picture is clear and encourages you to do something;
- the writing is clear and tells you either what to do or what not to do;
- the written message is direct.

The children again do a draft version of their sign before checking it with their group members, using photocopiable page 51 to evaluate its effectiveness. They then complete a final copy of the sign and display it in the appropriate place.

7

MAKING OUR SIGNS: EXPLAINING AND INFORMING

†††† ⏱60

Teaching content

Designing signs which are clear, concise and can be understood. Testing these on our friends. Key features of signs which give information.

What you need

Photocopiable pages 50, 51 and 48, blue highlighter pens, scrap paper, card, pencils, crayons, felt-tipped pens, paints, chalkboard.

What to do

This session takes the same form as the previous two sessions, except that this time the children identify and highlight in blue signs which will tell people information.

Model an example and clarify its key features. For example, if you use a sign such as that in Figure 4 ask the children what makes this an effective sign.

Figure 4

Try to elicit that:
- the picture is clear and shows a ticket;
- the writing is big, bold and simple;
- the sign is not overloaded;
- the arrow shows you where to go.

The children carry out this part of the session in the same way as before. They complete a draft version of their sign, ask their group members to evaluate it using photocopiable page 51 and then complete a final version. They then display it in its appropriate place.

8

ARE OUR SIGNS USEFUL?

ⓦ→†††† ⏱60

Teaching content

We can test our signs to see if they are effective.

What you need

Photocopiable page 52, volunteers (staff members, visitors, parents, other pupils), writing materials, paper, chalkboard.

What to do

Each group should now have designed and displayed their signs in the appropriate areas. Explain to the class that in order to check if their signs are useful to others they need to test them. Take some suggestions as to how this might be done. The children will probably suggest that they should try them out on other people.

Introduce the idea of someone with a problem. For example:

'I'm a father and I forgot to give Jamie his packed lunch this morning. I've checked with the headteacher and she says I can take it to Jamie's class. It is Room 10 and the teacher is Ms Balfour.'

Ask the children whether their signs would help this dad to find Jamie's class. How? See if they can suggest other problems which people in the school community might have and discuss these. Some examples may include:
• You are a visitor who wants to find the school office.
• You are a parent with a toddler who needs to find a toilet.
• You arrive in your car and want to find the main entrance to the school.
• You need to put your crisp bag in the bin at playtime.
• You want to know whose turn it is for the football pitch today.
• You've lost a glove. Where will you go?
• What's for dinner today?
• Where do I pay for my school dinner?
• How many people can play in the house?
• Which days are gym days?
• I've cut my finger. What should I do?

Copy some problems to test on to the board. The ones given above can be adapted to ones which will be relevant to the signs your pupils have made. Number the problems and ask the children to select the problems which their signs would help to solve. For example, they may have noted that there was an absence of signs in the playground showing where litter could be disposed of. Ask the children to write and number their problems on a sheet of paper. Explain to the children that you have asked for volunteers to test the signs and these problems are the ones they are going to test on their volunteers.

Invite the volunteers into the classroom and allocate one volunteer to each group. The children will give one problem at a time to the volunteer. The volunteer should read it out and then try to solve it using the children's signs displayed around the school. Explain the evaluation form on photocopiable page 52 to the groups and the volunteer.

Tell the group to accompany the volunteer around the school and to use the evaluation form at the end to assess the usefulness of their signs. The volunteers should assist the children in completing the evaluation form, especially the comments section.

On return to the classroom ask each group to report on the success of their signs. They may decide that some signs need to be refined or placed in a different position.

By sharing the evaluation information the children will see the success and real purpose and value of their signs. Seeing their signs around the school should give them a good sense of achievement.

SIGNS AND NOTICES

Scholastic
NON-FICTION WRITING PROJECTS
Workshop

WHY WE NEED SIGNS

1. To tell people information

2. To tell people to be careful

3. To tell people to do something

4. To tell people the rules

5. To persuade people to buy something

SIGNS WE NEED

We went to	
We need a sign to...	Where exactly?
1.	1.
2.	2.
3.	3.
4.	4.
5.	5.

DO MY SIGNS WORK?

Week 1	Yes (✓)	No (X)
Is the picture clear?		
Is the writing clear?		
Do you know what it is telling you?		
How could I improve it?		

Week 2	Yes (✓)	No (X)
Is the picture clear?		
Is the writing clear?		
Do you know what it is telling you?		
How could I improve it?		

Week 3	Yes (✓)	No (X)
Is the picture clear?		
Is the writing clear?		
Do you know what it is telling you?		
How could I improve it?		

EVALUATION FORM

Problem number	Found the sign Yes (✓) No (✗)	Used the sign Yes (✓) No (✗)	Solved the problem Yes (✓) No (✗)	Comments

Scholastic
WORKSHOP

Chapter Five

OUR GOOD TOY GUIDE

INTRODUCTION

Project description

In this project children compile a Good Toy Guide. This involves them in exploring the teacher's and each other's favourite toy, discussing why these toys are favourites, and deciding on the qualities which make them so special. The children consider what makes a good toy. This requires them to categorise toys in different ways. The project encourages children to collaborate in selecting categories and qualities, and to justify the inclusion of each toy in the guide. They test the toys against criteria devised by themselves to decide whether they should be included. The best toy in each category is selected for the Good Toy Guide.

Why this context?

Children like toys, but not all children like all toys or the same toys. They will often have very particular individual preferences. These preferences are influenced by a combination of factors, such as TV advertising, their friends, parents – in both positive and negative ways – and by their own personalities and lifestyles. The context of toys provides interest and motivation. Producing a Good Toy Guide provides children with opportunities to explore toys, to learn about categorising, to identify key features, to develop methods of fair testing and to select their preferences on the basis of criteria the children themselves have established.

Children's functional writing skills are naturally developed as they undertake a number of activities, such as labelling, developing suitable criteria for testing, testing using the criteria and organising the guide.

During the project children will look at commercial toy catalogues and use what they learn from these to organise their own guide with a cover, contents page and information pages.

Project organisation

While the whole class is involved in the project, the collaborative work is undertaken by mixed ability groups. Establishing these groups from the outset then letting them remain as working groups throughout the project is best. Class work is also important as the teacher models many of the important activities children carry out. Opportunities for sharing what has been found out and decisions made are vital. The whole class contribute to the end-product – a Good Toy Guide.

Publication, celebration and review

The Good Toy Guide will be published with illustrations or pictures, descriptions of the toys, test results, star ratings and prices. Pages of the guide should be A4 cartridge paper with one page allocated to each toy and its information. The number of pages will depend on the number of toys selected by the children for inclusion in the guide. The guide should be given to parents, grandparents or other children when they are selecting a toy as a gift for birthdays, Christmas or other celebrations in order to help them make their decisions.

fact that these may be some of the things that a good toy should be.

On a strip of paper write the heading 'A good toy should be...'. Attach the heading and the strips of paper to the wall for later use and further additions.

For the next session, ask the children to bring to school either their favourite toy or a photograph or picture of it. If they do not have one ask them to think about what their favourite toy would be.

2
MY FAVOURITE TOY

Teaching content

Toys can be grouped together and labelled. Toys in the same category share key features.

What you need

Children's favourite toys or pictures of them, key features from Session 1 (attached to the wall), folded A4 card for labelling, strips of paper, marker pen, writing and drawing materials, A4 paper.

What to do

Remind the children that you asked them to bring to school their favourite toy. Tell them to place these in front of them on their tables. Explore with some children why a particular toy is their favourite. If new key features are given, write these on strips of paper and attach them to the wall alongside the others identified in the previous session. At an appropriate point, draw the children's attention to these.

Give each child a sheet of A4 paper and tell them that you would like them to draw a picture of their favourite toy. Explain that while they are doing this you will be visiting them to find out why it is their favourite. Tell the children they should leave enough space underneath their picture to write four reasons why the toy is their favourite (or they can write them on the back of their sheet). They can refer to the reasons already listed on the wall if they need ideas. You may need to scribe for some children. As you move among the children, encourage them to add new reasons to the key features that have already been identified and placed on the wall.

1
TEACHER'S FAVOURITE TOY

Teaching content

We can give reasons why something is our favourite. We can identify key features of a good toy.

What you need

Strips of paper, marker pen, a favourite toy or a photograph of it.

What to do

Bring the class together and tell the children that you have brought in something very special to show them. Explain that it is something you enjoy playing with, for example a pack of cards or an item associated with a sport, or enjoyed playing with as a child, such as a cuddly toy. It is or was your favourite toy. Show the children your item or photograph.

Tell the children there are several good reasons why it is your favourite toy. Ask them if they can guess what these are. Listen to the children's suggestions and write them on strips of paper. For example, 'It was good to cuddle'.

Ask questions to encourage the children to identify possible reasons why the toy is your favourite and to give their reasons also. When the children have exhausted their ideas, recap the suggestions they made, highlighting the

When the children have completed this part of the session, draw their attention again to the list of key features and tell them they are going to test these out. Select a toy, for example a racing car, and highlight the key features in relation to this toy. For example:

Is it good to look at? **Yes**
Is it good to cuddle? **No**
Is it good for playing with other people? **Yes**
Is it strong and won't break easily? **Yes**
Does it build lots of things? **No**

Establish with the children that the key features they have identified are important but that not all of them are relevant to every kind of toy. Stress that there are different kinds of toys and these can be classified in different ways – toys to cuddle, toys to build with, toys for babies, and so on. When you feel the children have understood this, organise them into groups and tell them to sort the toys they have brought in into different kinds, using the criteria you have just explained. Tell the children that different people in the group may have different ideas about how the toys should be categorised and they will have to discuss, listen to one another and come to a decision.

When each group has sorted their toys, hand out blank labels made from folded A4 card. Tell the groups to decide on a name for each of their sets or categories of toys, and write out a label for each name, for example 'cars', 'cuddlies', 'dolls'.

To conclude this session, ask each group to tell the class how they classified their toys and what they called each category. Display the labels and the children's drawings.

CLASSIFYING TOYS
††††→ⓦ→†††† ⏱⁶⁰

Teaching content
Toys can be classified in different ways by different people. Reasons can be given as to why they were classified in a particular way. You can appreciate other people's way of doing it as being different but not incorrect.

What you need
A selection of toys, or pictures of toys, for each group (including a doll, an action man, building game, ball, skipping rope, cuddly toy, rattle, toy car, pull along toy, bucket and spade – ensure that the selection encompasses toys for various ages, interests and genders), a selection of toy catalogues – one per group, A4 card for labelling, two sheets of sugar paper per group, adhesive, scissors, chalkboard, large sheet of card, marker pens.

What to do
Ask the children to work in the same groups as before and give each group a selection of toys, or pictures of toys, from those that you have gathered. Ask them to sort these into different categories. Remind the children that different people in the group may have different ideas as to how the toys should be classified so they must listen to each other. There is not just one way to do it!

Allow the children about 15 minutes for this task. Monitor their progress and be on hand to

Scholastic
NON-FICTION WRITING PROJECTS
Workshop

Toys for babies

Construction – toys

a class the way in which toys could be classified for the Good Toy Guide. Record suggestions and ideas on a large sheet of card for display. Having decided on the categories, for example 'toys for babies', 'construction toys', 'cars', 'dolls', 'pull-along toys', 'cuddly toys', allocate two categories to each group, making sure that each group has different categories. Issue each group with two sheets of sugar paper and tell them to label each sheet with their category headings.

Explain that the Good Toy Guide will be looking at toys from all these categories. Ask, 'What kind of toys will fit in each?'

Ask the children to cut out relevant pictures from their catalogues and stick these on to their sheets. For example, a picture of a rattle would be placed under the toys for babies category, pictures of bricks under construction toys. Display the finished sheets on the wall.

4

DESIGNING TOY TESTS

Teaching content
Deciding three key features of toys in different categories. Checking, through testing and discussion, that these are the three most sensible. Discussing suggestions with each other.

What you need
Two toys for each category identified in the previous session, list of key features (attached to the wall from Session 1), large sheet of paper divided into rectangular boxes, photocopiable page 64, writing and drawing materials.

What to do
Tell the children that before toys can be included in their Good Toy Guide they must make sure that they are good toys. They must test them. Ask the children what sort of qualities they should test the toys for. Suggest that the list of key features of a good toy that they have created may be helpful in ascertaining this.

Remind the children that some qualities and features are suitable for some toys but not for others. Explain that they are going to decide on the three most important characteristics of the toys in their categories. Model an example with the children, for instance construction toys.

help with ideas and arguments if necessary. Ask the children to write label cards for each category of toy that they have identified, in the same way as they did in the previous session. Help with scribing if necessary.

Bring the class back together and discuss the variety of ways in which toys can be classified. Explore issues as they arise. For example, a gender issue may arise out of the questions, 'Is an action man a doll? Are there boys' and girls' toys?' Introduce the idea of making a Good Toy Guide or catalogue that will inform people which toys are good. Highlight the fact that such a guide would need a method of classifying toys and that guides need to be organised so that people can find the toys and pages they want quickly.

Discuss with the children how toy catalogues might classify their toys. Give each group a toy catalogue, and ask them to investigate how their catalogue has classified its toys. When they are ready each group should report orally what they have found.

Identify similarities and differences between the children's classifications decided in the previous session, those decided in this session and the catalogues' classifications. Consider as

Ask the group that was allocated construction toys to play with some construction toys for two minutes while the other children watch. At the end of the time ask the class what they feel, through having played with and observed the toys, are the important features of construction toys. Encourage them to refer to the key features list. The answers will probably include: they are strong; they fit together well; they can make lots of things. Record these points on the large sheet of paper, writing each point in a separate box.

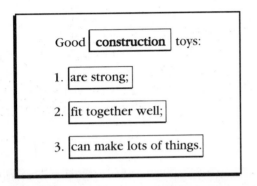

You may prefer to draw appropriate pictures to explain these key points if you are working with very young children. See Figure 1.

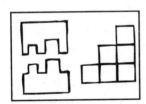

Figure 1

Explain to the children that you want them to use the same process to establish the key features of the toys in their categories. If they have been allocated toys for babies and cars, for example, they will work with these to decide on their key qualities. Give the children some toys relating to the various categories and tell them to play with them for a while in order to establish their most important features. While they are working, the children should discuss with each other what the most important characteristics are. When they have decided on the three most important qualities, give each group a copy of photocopiable page 64. Explain that in the first three boxes they should write down the three important qualities they have

identified. For example:

Good baby toys
1. are cuddly;
2. are bright to look at;
3. make a noise.

Good toddler toys
1. are strong;
2. can be pushed or pulled;
3. are bright to look at.

Good dolls
1. are good for playing with friends;
2. have nice clothes to wear;
3. have hair to brush.

Good toy cars
1. go fast;
2. are strong;
3. are good for playing with friends.

In the remaining three boxes the children can draw pictures to illustrate what they have written.

These 'good toy' sheets identify the three key criteria against which children will test each toy in their category. Tell the groups to share their decisions at the end of the session.

5

INTRODUCING A GOOD TOY TEST

Teaching content

How to show information you find out. How to compare and contrast different toys.

What you need

A range of toys from each category (the children may help to supply these from home), photocopiable page 65 (plus an enlarged copy for demonstration with the class), writing materials.

What to do

Tell the class that they are going to use the information they researched in the previous session, in which they identified the three most important features of the toys in their categories. Tell them that they will be completing a Good

Toy Test sheet so that toys can be tested fairly one against the other.

Model an example, for instance toy cars, using your enlarged copy of photocopiable page 65. Explain that if it was decided that the three important features of a toy car were its speed, its strength and whether or not it was good for playing with friends, then the children will need to work out a method of testing these points and recording the results. Explain the design of the photocopiable sheet to the children – there are spaces for the name of the category of toy, the name of the specific toy, a picture of it, the criteria that have been identified (from the previous session) and its star rating.

Ask one group to test a toy car while the rest of the class watches. Take each point in turn. For example:

• Speed – two children should race their car and decide if it goes:

    very fast – 2 stars
    quite fast – 1 star
    slow – 0 star

Tick the appropriate box.

• Strength – two children should play with the car and devise a test to decide how strong the car is. They may bring their own experiences to bear and consider what the car is made of, whether it has any loose parts, whether it would break if stood on or if it crashed. They should then decide if it is:

    very strong – 2 stars
    OK for strength – 1 star
    not strong – 0 star

Again tick the appropriate box.

• Good for playing with a friend – two children

should play together with the car and decide if it is:

    great for playing with a friend – 2 stars
    OK for playing with a friend – 1 star
    not very good for playing with a friend – 0 star

Ask a child to tick the appropriate box.

The children then count up the total number of stars and add this to the star rating box. The group now decide on one best feature of the toy car and write this in the box at the bottom of the sheet. For example, 'The best thing about this toy is it is very fast and very strong'. Discuss the sheet with the class and then display it.

This modelling helps the children to understand how to use the criteria they identified in the previous session and recorded on photocopiable page 64. Give each group a copy of photocopiable page 65 and set them to work on the toys in their categories. Be on hand to monitor, scribe and help when required, making sure that all the children understand what they are doing.

During the next few days either at worktime or choosing time the children, in pairs or small groups, should be encouraged to take a copy of photocopiable page 65 and carry out tests on the selection of toys in their categories. They may also wish to take one or more sheets to test their toys or their family's toys at home.

Each group will have collected test results and star ratings for a range of toys in their two categories. These test results will be used in the next session. The three highest scoring toys in each category will be included in the children's Good Toy Guide.

THE GOOD TOYS

Teaching content

What information do we need to give? What is the best way to give it?

What you need

Three highest scoring test sheets for toys in each category, paper and felt-tipped pens, selection of toy catalogues and pictures of toys, paper, writing materials, Blu-Tack, photocopiable pages 65 and 66 (plus an enlarged copy of both for demonstration with the class).

What to do

Gather the class together and read them the information given in a catalogue or toy guide about a toy. Repeat this for another toy, encouraging the children to think about the type of information given. See how many things they can list orally that are included in catalogue information. This would include:

- the price;
- the size and colour – what the toy looks like;
- the age-group it is aimed at or would be suitable for;
- what it does (if applicable).

Establish with the children that this is the type of information they will need to include in their Good Toy Guide.

Select one group's completed photocopiable sheet from the previous session and the appropriate toy. Introduce your enlarged copy of photocopiable page 66 and model how it is used. Work through the sheet in the following way:

1. Fill in the name of the toy category (for example, cars).
2. Provide a picture of the toy. This could be a drawing, a catalogue picture or a photograph.
3. Transfer the information from photocopiable page 65 to the section 'This toy is good because', using the criteria investigated. For example, under the category of toy cars, its key features were identified as being its speed, its strength and that it is good for playing with friends.
4. Transfer the star rating.
5. Transfer the information from 'The best thing about this toy is' to the section 'Our testers said'.
6. Decide on a suitable price for the toy, based on the children's knowledge and some sample catalogue prices.

Explain that the number space at the top of the sheet will be filled in later.

Tell the children to choose a partner from their group and give each pair a copy of photocopiable page 66. Tell them to choose one of their test sheets and to transfer the information on to the photocopiable sheet you have just given them in the same way that you have just done. (Make sure that the three highest scoring test sheets for each category each have their information transferred.) Remind the children to leave the number space blank for the time being as this will be filled in during another session.

This task could be completed at choosing time, worktime or during a writing session.

As these sheets will form the pages of the Good Toy Guide it may be necessary to allow the children to do a rough draft first, then a final copy.

As pairs of children complete their task, attach the sheets to the wall for reference, at an appropriate height for the children to reach in a later session.

7

FRONT AND BACK COVERS
††††-ⓦ-†††† ⏱60

Teaching content

The front and back covers of books carry standard information which includes title, author and publisher. There may also be pictures, as well as biographical details and a brief description of the book.

What you need

Selection of non-fiction books (enough to give each group three books), two rectangles of card slightly larger than A4, drawing paper, felt-tipped pens, writing materials, scrap paper, adhesive, chalkboard or large sheet of paper.

What to do

Organise the children into their groups and give each group some scrap paper and three non-fiction books from the selection you have gathered. Tell them to look at the books carefully and think about what information is given on the front cover. Give them some scrap paper and ask them to write a list of their ideas. Allow the children some time to do this and then take feedback from the groups, recording their suggestions on the board or a large sheet of paper. Ensure that the list includes the facts that the cover contains:
• the title of the story or book;
• the author's name;
• a picture or illustration which suggests the content of the book.

Follow a similar procedure for the back cover, ensuring that the list includes the facts that the back cover contains:
• comments from critics, reviewers or magazines.
• biographical details of the author.
• a short description of the book written in a concise manner.

Working with the class, build up an example showing how a front and back cover could be created for the Good Toy Guide.

For instance, on the front cover would be:
• the book title – Our Good Toy Guide;
• the author's name – Class 3 or Primary 1;
• a picture or illustration – one toy from each category.

On the back cover would be:
• comments from critics/reviewers – short positive statements;
• author details – picture of the group or class and information about them;
• a short description – what the book is about

Explain to the groups that their task is to complete a front and back cover. This can be assigned, for example, as follows:
• the book title – one child could write this on a strip of paper;
• the author – another child could write the class's name on a strip of paper;
• the illustration – several children could draw or cut out a picture of a toy to use as the illustration;
• comments from critics/reviewers – several children could write these.
• the author details – one child from each group could write the author details;
• the short description – a pair of children could write this.

When the children have finished their contributions, they should attach the various pieces of writing and the illustration on to the pieces of A4 card in order to create the front and back covers for their editions of the Good Toy Guide. Store these for later use.

PUTTING IT TOGETHER

Teaching content
When compiling a book you need to think about ordering then numbering the pages.

What you need
Good Toy Sheets attached to the wall from Session 6, front and back covers created in the previous session, marker pen, strips of card for labelling, writing materials.

What to do
Gather the class together and look at the children's completed versions of photocopiable page 66, which you attached to the wall at the end of Session 6.

Ask the children to suggest ideas as to how these could be sequenced for the Good Toy Guide. They should recognise that all toys from the same category, for instance construction toys, should go together. Decide with the children which category of toys should be first, second, third, and so on. Rearrange the pages on the wall, using strips of card to label each category.

When this is completed, ask a child to write the appropriate numbers in the Good Toy number boxes at the top of the sheets starting at number one for the first toy in the first category and continuing sequentially to the last toy in the final category.

Ask another child to number each page in order, writing the appropriate number in the bottom centre of the sheet.

Leave this material on display until required in the next session.

CONTENTS PAGE

Teaching content
The Good Toy Guide needs a contents page so that readers can find the information they want quickly and easily.

What you need
Selection of information books, photocopiable page 67 (plus an enlarged copy for demonstration with the class), copies of the children's completed photocopiable page 66, marker pen, stapler, adhesive, writing materials, ribbon.

What to do
Note: Prior to this session you will need to make copies of the children's completed Good Toy Guide sheets that have been attached to the wall. Each group will need one copy of each sheet.

Gather the children around the wall display where the numbered pages of the Good Toy

Guide have been arranged in order. Explain to the children that people looking at an information book, especially a catalogue, often want to find the information they are looking for quickly. Ask the children if they can think of how some books help you to do this. They may suggest a contents page. If not, demonstrate this from the selection of information books you have available. Point out to the children that:
• The information on a contents page should be short and clear.
• The page numbers are given beside the information.

Confirm with the children that the information they want to give on their contents page is the category of toy.

Introduce your enlarged version of photocopiable page 67. Select individuals to take turns in completing the sections, using the information from the wall display. For example:

| baby toys | p.1 | or | pp.1–3 |
| toddler toys | p.2 | or | pp.4–7 |

Explain that the box next to the heading is for the children to attach or draw a suitable picture.

Give each group a copy of photocopiable page 67 and tell them to complete it. Depending on how many categories there are the children may need two or several copies of this photocopiable sheet.

When the contents pages are completed, give each group their copy of the completed Good Toy Guide sheets and tell them to place them between their front and back covers to make up their copies of the Good Toy Guide. These can be stapled together or punched and tied with ribbon.

10

TESTING OUR GOOD TOY GUIDE

Teaching content
The Good Toy Guide has a purpose: to help people choose a good gift for a child. We need to test whether it serves this purpose.

What you need
Copies of the Good Toy Guide, photocopiable page 68, volunteers (such as teachers, parents, grandparents, children).

What to do
Gather the class together and remind the children of the purpose of their Good Toy Guide. Explain that the only way they can find out if it does what it is supposed to do is to test it out.

Encourage the children to suggest a person to test it out on. This may be in school or at home. List their suggestions for volunteers on the board or a large sheet of paper.

Show the children photocopiable page 68, explaining the questions and layout. The children can then, over a period of a few days, work in pairs using this to evaluate the effectiveness of their Good Toy Guide by testing it out on their volunteers.

Take some time to discuss the feedback noted on photocopiable page 68 before using the information gathered to adapt and improve the guide. Final versions of the guide may be placed in the school library, local library, doctor's surgery, parents' room, and so on.

To bring the project to a satisfying conclusion it might be appropriate to invite the headteacher to visit the classroom to learn about what the children did and how their guide was received by others. Alternatively it might be possible to invite the manager of a local toy store to visit the classroom and present him or her with a Good Toy Guide.

TESTING OUR TOYS

Good _____ toys:

1.

2.

3.

1.

2.

3.

THE GOOD TOY TEST

The Good Toy Test for:	Name of toy:

Picture of toy:

Comments	★★	★	No stars
1.			
2.			
3.			

Star rating for this toy is

The best thing about this toy is

THE GOOD TOYS

Good Toy Number

Name:

Stick a picture of the toy here

This toy is good because

Star rating

Our testers said

Price

CONTENTS PAGE

_____toys

p._____

_____toys

p._____

_____toys

p._____

_____toys

p._____

EVALUATION SHEET

Does our Good Toy Guide work?	☺	☹
Did you:		
• find the guide easy to use?		
• like the cover?		
• find the information helpful?		
• find a toy you wanted to buy?		
How could we make it better? Thank you for helping us.		

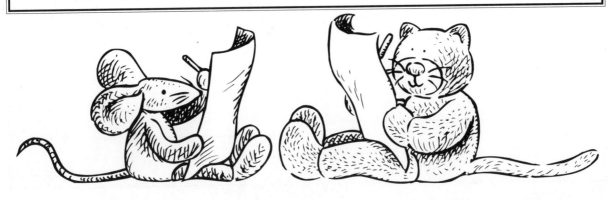

Scholastic
NON-FICTION WRITING PROJECTS
Workshop

Scholastic WORKSHOP

Chapter Six

WEATHER STATION

INTRODUCTION

Project description

In this project, the children respond to a request from the headteacher to investigate how well their schoolmates protect themselves from inclement weather. They address questions such as 'Do older children dress more suitably than younger children? Do different age groups prefer different types of weather?' Children can also extend the project to run a campaign to increase awareness of the importance of dressing appropriately.

The teacher and class can negotiate exactly which activities they wish to do during the project. The work may involve keeping a weather diary over three weeks for background information; surveying the various classes in the school and then writing reports on how they feel about different weather conditions or what they wore on a particular day and how suitable this was; interviewing children and parents to report on the debates that different age groups have at home about what to wear. As a result of what they have discovered, the children may choose to design posters to persuade people to dress more appropriately or advertise an award for the most suitably dressed class.

The project culminates in the children organising a school assembly or a display in the entrance hall. Evaluation and review is undertaken on one main piece of work, which is chosen by the child and explained and discussed in group meetings with the headteacher. Written responses and comments are provided by the headteacher and, if required, by other groups in the school.

Why this project?

What to wear to school is an issue of debate in many homes. The project deals with genuine questions: Are some age groups more suitably dressed than others and, if so, why? What are the attitudes of parents and children towards dressing for school and do the same issues arise irrespective of age or gender?

This project provides plenty of opportunities for the teacher to model and directly teach aspects of report writing, and for the children to revisit and practise the ideas, perhaps with less teacher input in a range of activities. It also illustrates how, when one format – a poster – is used for different purposes, the language, structure and planning strategies may be different.

Project organisation

The project has been designed to be carried out with the whole class. Although, for the purposes of organising the project, the children are allocated to fairly large groups, each of which is given a class to investigate, all the written tasks are undertaken by children working individually or in pairs. The larger groups serve as a focus for quite tightly structured discussion and can be reconfigured to allow individual or paired work to be collated into group reports.

Obviously, at the start of the project it is necessary for the class teacher to secure the involvement of the headteacher and to arrange convenient times for the children to visit other classes to carry out their surveys and investigations. If parents are to be interviewed, the teacher will need to contact them at an appropriate point in the project.

Decisions about whether to disseminate the project results via a school assembly or a display in the main entrance to the school will need to be negotiated well in advance to allow everyone time to organise this.

Publication, celebration and review

This project results in a number of different types of publications, depending on the activities chosen – information charts, reports, posters and presentations. Review and evaluation takes place during each activity as the children work together and when they present and explain their reports to their peers in order to collate a group report on the whole school.

The final celebration and review is carried out on a specific piece of work, chosen by the child, which is explained and discussed with a group of peers and the headteacher.

Books the children may find useful

Weather, Kay Davies and Wendy Oldfield (1993) Wayland
Wind and Rain, Claire Llewellyn and Anthony Lewis (1996) Hamlyn
Day and Night, Claire Llewellyn and Anthony Lewis (1996) Hamlyn
Weather, Sally Morgan (1995) Wayland
Weather, John Farndon (1992) Dorling Kindersley
My Science Book of Weather, Neil Ardley (1992) Dorling Kindersley

WEATHER INQUIRIES

W 45

Teaching content

The introduction to a letter must indicate the topic and set a polite and courteous tone. The middle section explains the issues in more detail. Letters often end by inviting further comment or action. Letters with similar purposes often share a similar structure.

What you need

Photocopiable page 81, chalkboard, poster-sized sheet of paper, marker pens, writing materials.

What to do

Gather the class together and tell them that they have received a letter from the headteacher which you will read aloud. Read the letter on photocopiable page 81 (or a version of it adapted to the needs of your class).

Each of the activities suggested in the headteacher's letter is described by a session in this project. You may negotiate with your class which activities to carry out.

Discuss the headteacher's letter with the children. Write the key questions and the suggested activities mentioned in the letter on the board. Ask the class which questions they find interesting and would enjoy investigating. For example: Do the children think that older pupils are more suitably dressed than younger ones? Do they think that older or younger pupils have more arguments about what to wear? Who do they think makes the final decisions? Which of the activities listed would the children find most interesting to carry out? Why?

Give the children a few minutes to discuss these issues with someone sitting nearby before taking feedback from the whole class.

From the class discussion, elicit a clear set of questions and activities the children might like to carry out. Discuss a suitable sequence for these activities and record this on the poster-sized sheet of paper. This can be displayed in the classroom throughout the project, providing a constant reminder of the focus and sequence of work.

Explain that the class will have to draft a reply to the headteacher's letter. Model the response with the whole class. Ask the children for suggestions about how their reply should begin. Explain that the headteacher receives many letters each day. The introduction to their letter therefore must remind him or her of the topic and indicate that this is a reply. Emphasise the importance throughout of being polite and courteous. The middle section of the letter should explain what the class are prepared to do and why they think this is an interesting approach. Finally, the letter should end in a courteous and pleasant manner and invite further comment if required. If appropriate, encourage the children to note the similarities in structure between the letter they have just written and that sent to their class by the headteacher.

In modelling the reply, encourage the children

to contribute their own ideas in their own words. Model how writers reread what has been written, and explain that they can add, delete or change words, phrases or sentences so that they are redrafting as they write. Then choose one or two children to write a fair copy of the letter, on headed paper, which will be sent to the headteacher.

You may also like to make a photocopy of the children's letter to display on the classroom wall alongside the headteacher's original letter.

WEATHER WATCH

IconTeaching content
Symbols can be used to give clear and quick information; patterns and generalisations need to be explained in words.

What you need
Photocopiable page 82, writing and drawing materials, A4 paper, chalkboard.

What to do
Gather the class together. Explain that a weather record will provide useful background information for the class investigations. It will supply information about how variable the weather is from day-to-day and about how the pattern varies over several weeks.

Suggest the children work in pairs to build up a weather record over a three-week period. Begin by asking the class to brainstorm the different weather conditions that may occur. They will probably suggest words such as 'rain', 'sunshine', 'windy', 'snowy', 'thunder and lightning', 'fog', 'mist'. Write these on the board so that the children can refer to them. Explain that some of these are absolute conditions (thunder and lightning, for example) but that others may vary. The rain, for instance, may be a light drizzle or a downpour, snow might be a few flakes or a complete whiteout, and the wind may be a light breeze or a hurricane!

Organise the children into pairs and give them some paper and drawing materials. Ask them to devise symbols to represent the weather words they have listed. Explain that the important feature of symbols is that they are

simple and easily distinguishable from each other. Ask them to decide which weather conditions may vary in intensity and see if they can incorporate some indication of this into their symbols. They may, for example, decide to indicate the strength of the rain by altering the number of raindrops they draw, changing the colour of the cloud or raindrops, incorporating a numerical value into the symbol, and so on.

When they have done this, bring the class together and ask individual pairs to explain some of the symbols they have chosen and why. Give each pair a copy of photocopiable page 82 and explain that they should make any changes they wish to clarify the symbols they have devised before drawing their symbols in the boxes provided at the top of the sheet.

When they have done this, explain to the whole class how to complete the weather record chart on photocopiable page 82. Tell the children to take turns to discuss and record the weather conditions each day. Using their symbols, they should then draw the appropriate one in the correct box. Bring the children's attention to the sentence at the bottom of the sheet and explain that they will only be able to complete this when they have filled in the whole chart in three weeks' time.

Once the charts have been completed or are well underway, discuss the various symbols chosen and make a class display to show the range of representations used.

When the charts are finally completed, put the children into groups of four and ask them to compare their charts. Ask:

• Do the two charts always agree? If not, why do they think this is the case?

• Can they complete the sentence at the bottom of the photocopiable sheet? Is this the sentence they would have written had they not kept a record?

• Were the weather symbols the children devised similar? If not, were they equally clear and easy to use? What were the advantages/disadvantages of each?

• Would the children do anything different next time? If so, what?

Call the class together. Ask different groups to report back on the various issues. Encourage them to articulate what they have learned about:

• choosing and using symbols;

• making generalisations and stating these clearly.

End the session by telling the children the charts will be used as part of a display or assembly, whichever they decide to do.

Further development

Poster-sized versions of the charts can be made for display in an assembly or entrance hall.

3

WEATHER PREFERENCES

Teaching content

Reports begin by stating the topic and the specific question(s) that will be addressed. They make generalised statements about the topic in question. The use of headings can make the report clearer and easier to write.

What you need

Photocopiable page 83, poster-sized sheet of paper, marker pen, writing and drawing materials.

What to do

Remind the children that the headteacher suggested it would be interesting to find out whether children in different age-groups have distinct preferences regarding particular types of weather, or if everyone has similar likes and dislikes.

Distribute photocopiable page 83 to each child. Explain that the children will be using this to carry out a survey of each class in the school, beginning with themselves. Show the children how to complete the sheet and allow about ten minutes for them to do this.

(*Note*: The sheet can be simplified by giving the

Finally, tell the children that you have arranged for them to visit other classes to conduct the survey. Divide the class into groups so that each group can focus on one class. Explain that each group will (at a suitable time to be negotiated with the class teacher) visit the class, introduce themselves, describe the purpose of the survey, explain the format of the photocopiable sheet and ask each child to give his or her opinion of one of the weather conditions on the sheet. Six children will therefore contribute to one photocopiable sheet.

When the children have completed their surveys, ask them to work individually or in pairs to write a series of short statements about the views of the class they surveyed. Each individual/pair should write about *one* of the weather conditions listed. These can then be collated to form a group report. Remind the children of the importance of having suitable headings for each section of their report and suggest the group works together to draft a joint introduction.

children a smaller number of decisions on which to report – simply cut the sheet to omit the final two weather conditions.)

Draw each of the weather pictures (heavy rain, bright sunshine, and so on) underneath each other on the poster-sized paper, using lines to separate them. Ask the children to indicate with a show of hands which emotions they recorded for each weather type. Record this as a series of simple statements next to the appropriate sections. You might, for example, write:

Snow: 10 people in Class ___ think 'Oh no, yuk' when they see the snow. 15 people in Class ___ think 'Yipadee doo dah!' when they see the snow.

Explain that if this information is to be presented in the form of a written report, the children will need to write a short introduction to the topic, explaining the specific issue that has been addressed and why it is interesting, so that it makes sense to a reader who does not know the context. Ask the children to work in pairs to draft a suitable introduction. When they have completed this, select some pairs to share their introductions with the rest of the class.

Explain that the use of headings makes the report clear and easy to write. Demonstrate how the single weather words can be made into meaningful headings, such as 'What do Class ___ think of snowy weather?' or 'Class ___'s opinions on snow'.

4

WHAT DID YOU WEAR TODAY?

Teaching content

Reports begin by stating the topic and the specific question(s) that will be addressed. They make generalised statements about the topic in question. The use of headings can make the report clearer and easier to write.

What you need

Photocopiable page 84, writing materials, scrap paper, chalkboard.

What to do

Remind the children of why they thought the topic of different clothing for different weather conditions was an interesting and important issue to investigate. Ask them whether they think there will be a considerable difference in how suitably the different age-groups dress for the weather, and ask them to predict (with a show of hands) which class they think will be most suitably dressed.

Organise the children into groups. Allocate each group a class to survey (including their own class) and give each group a copy of photocopiable page 84 to read and some scrap paper. Explain that first the children must decide as a class on the ideal items of clothing for children to have worn on their way to school that day. Give the groups a few minutes to discuss this and ask them to draw or write their list on the scrap paper provided. When the prescribed time is up, ask each group to appoint a spokesperson to report their group's decision to the rest of the class. Record each group's suggestions on the board. Encourage the class to discuss any discrepancies between the suggestions offered until all the class agree and final decisions on the items of clothing are made. Then ask each group to record these items on their photocopiable sheet by drawing or writing *one* item in each box. So, for example, if it was a rainy day they might draw a raincoat, wellingtons, umbrella, hat, jumper, and various other appropriate items.

Tell each group to appoint two ambassadors who will visit their allocated class, explain why they are gathering this information, and gather the appropriate information by asking for a show of hands for each item in turn, thus finding out how many people actually wore that item on their way to school that morning. Ensure the children understand that they are to record the results in the smaller boxes provided next to their drawings and that they appreciate the importance of counting carefully and writing clearly. (You may need to teach some strategies to ensure an accurate count. For example, you could suggest that they count the children table by table, each perform a separate count and compare results as a double check for accuracy, and so on.)

On their return, ask each group to appoint a spokesperson to report their results and record these as a chart on the board. List the items of clothing across the top and the classes in sequence down the left-hand side. Discuss the results with the class. What general or specific observations can the children make? Can the children detect any patterns? Which is the best/worst class for wearing particular items of clothing? Together, compile a class list of statements about the overall results.

Next organise the groups into two working groups with an ambassador working in each. Ask each working group to work in pairs and draft a report of their results. Remind them that their reports will need:

• an introduction which states the topic, why it is interesting or important and the specific question(s) that will be addressed;

• headings to make the report clear – these will also make it easier to write;

• clear statements of the results under the appropriate heading;

• a conclusion which indicates whether the class interviewed was in their opinion, on the whole, suitably dressed or not for the prevailing weather.

The following starter sentences may be supplied for children who need further support: Introduction: This report is about... It is important/interesting because... Our questions were...

Once finished, ask each pair to read their draft report to the rest of their group.

Organise the class into new groups so that each group contains children who have drafted reports on a different class. These can be combined to compile a report which covers the whole school. Finally, the groups can decide on a title for their report and write a final section by selecting and sequencing statements about the overall picture from the class list, remembering to choose an appropriate heading for this final section.

CLOTHING ARGUMENTS: WHO DECIDES?

Teaching content
Key questions can help to structure a report.

What you need
Writing materials, photocopiable page 85, chalkboard, parents.

What to do
Remind the children about why they thought it would be interesting to seek parents' and children's views about who decides what children should wear to school in different weather conditions, and why. With the class, brainstorm some interesting questions and list

these on the board. The children may suggest questions on the following issues:
• How do children come by their outdoor clothes? Are they 'passed down' from older children or bought new?
• Who decides or chooses which clothes to buy, or when a particular item of clothing is needed?
• Who decides each morning what the child will wear to school?
• Do children and parents always agree on what to wear?
• Which types of weather cause the most disagreement? Why?
• What happens when they disagree?
• How many different types of footwear do you have?
• Do you have an umbrella, scarf, hat, gloves?
• Do you have different types of coats?

Once a good range of questions has been generated, divide the children into pairs and ask them to choose three or four questions that they find most interesting and would like to ask. Tell them to list also general information that interviewers may wish to know, such as the name of the parent and the age of the child or children.

Arrange for several parents, preferably with children from different age-groups, to visit the class for approximately 10 minutes. Organise the children into groups so that each parent is speaking to approximately the same number of children. Tell the children to ask their questions and listen carefully to the answers. They should note down the parents' answers to their questions on a sheet of paper so that they can

refer to them later. Explain that some children may have similar questions so they must listen very carefully to each other so that they do not repeat the same question.

When the children have finished their interviewing, ask them to work individually and to write a report of their interview. You may need to remind them that their reports will require:
• an introduction which states the topic and why it is interesting or important and gives basic details about the interviewee;
• clear statements of the results under the appropriate heading.

Their report may end with a concluding statement which emphasises some of the interesting or important points that have been made. Explain that the children may or may not wish to use headings, but they will certainly have to give their report a clear title which indicates what it is about.

Support can be given to those who need it by using the sentence starters supplied for the previous session.

The individual reports can be collated into a class book. Children should be encouraged to read the book and complete one of the slips on photocopiable page 85, several copies of which can be stapled into the back of the book.

6
POSTER PERSUASION
w -ᵼᵼ 50

Teaching content
Posters may be written to persuade others. Effective persuasion often involves using recognised phrases and slogans to catch the readers' attention, putting forward a clear, simple message and sometimes thinking of arguments to counter the readers' likely viewpoint.

What you need
Poster-sized paper, scrap paper, writing, drawing and painting materials, chalkboard, books of weather sayings and songs.

What to do
Gather the class together and discuss how the weather enables them to enjoy different activities. For example, in snowy weather they

can build snowmen and go sledging; in sunny weather they can play football, have a picnic or get out the paddling pool; and in the rain they can splash in the puddles. Record some of their ideas in pictorial form on the board. Then point out that people will only enjoy each activity if they are suitably dressed for it – playing in the snow is miserable if your clothes are not warm enough; an outing on a sunny day can be ruined if you get sunburnt or are wearing heavy, thick clothes; and jumping in puddles loses its attraction if it means you spend the rest of the day in wet socks and shoes.

Explore key ideas about why it is important to wear suitable clothes for different weather conditions. Explain that being properly dressed can prevent illness, provide comfort, protect 'good' indoor clothes and ensure you spend the day looking smart and fashionable.

Ask the children why they think people do not always wear suitable clothing. They may give suggestions such as: people being thoughtless; not noticing the weather outside; rushing to get out and not having time to dress properly; not having (or being able to find) appropriate clothes; not wanting to carry clothes home should the weather improve, and so on.

Figure 1

> The weather we chose is: _____
>
> Two good things to do in this weather are:
>
> _____
>
> _____
>
> The slogan we will use is: _____
>
> _____
>
> Some good things to wear during this weather are:
>
> _____
>
> _____
>
> _____

Organise the children into pairs. Explain that they are going to make a poster which will persuade people to dress properly for a particular kind of weather. Ask each pair to decide what type of weather they wish to target.

Explain that effective persuasion often involves using recognised phrases and slogans to catch the readers' attention. Show the children the books containing weather sayings and songs. Suggest they look through these to find a suitable, short and catchy slogan relating to the weather condition they are targeting. Alternatively, brainstorm with the children weather sayings they may know or have heard. Give one or two examples, such as 'Rain, rain go away' 'Red sky at night, shepherds' delight'. Then tell them to think about enjoyable activities in this type of weather, what clothes should be worn to maximise the enjoyment and one or two really good reasons why. It might be helpful to generate a planning framework on the board. See Figure 1.

Explain that a persuasive poster puts forward a clear, simple message, presented in a strong visual format – bold colours, eye-catching drawings and short, concise language.

Give the children some scrap paper and allow them 15 minutes to discuss and decide the key message and layout of their poster. You may need to explain how to do this by giving them an example, showing that this first draft is an opportunity to 'rough out' their ideas and to make decisions on the size and position of the slogan, words and pictures. It does not require careful drawing or colouring.

It is often helpful to set a time-limit of 15 minutes for this rough draft. Warn the children when they have 5 minutes and 2 minutes left. At the end of the set drafting period give the children paper for them to make a fair copy of their poster. Again, you may need to set a time-limit.

Once finished, posters can be displayed in appropriate areas around the school. If possible, ask the children to choose where their poster should go.

Further development

The same approach can be used to make posters advertising the assembly or entrance hall display. Explain that, in as few words as possible, the poster needs to convey why the display/assembly will be interesting.

7
POSTER INFORMATION
†† 50

Teaching content

Information posters need to make the topic or question clear, give one or two key facts and indicate how to obtain further information. The language must be clear and concise.

What you need

Poster-sized paper, scrap paper, writing and drawing materials.

What to do

Organise the children into pairs. Ask them to pick *one* surprising fact that they have discovered during their work for this topic and to write this in as few words as possible.

Explain that information posters need to make the topic or question clear, give one or two key facts and indicate how to obtain further information. The language must be clear and concise and the heading must be eye-catching, perhaps indicating the topic or question (for example, 'What we wear to school', 'Who is the best dressed class?') or being less specific ('Did you know...?' 'Read and learn!').

Next ask the children to think about how

best to present and illustrate the interesting fact they have chosen. Remind them that their poster will also need to indicate how to obtain further information and they must leave space for this. Allow the children to explore their ideas on rough paper before making their poster. As in the previous session, you may need to demonstrate how the first draft is an opportunity to 'rough out' ideas and decide the size and position of the heading, exact wording and pictures. It does not require careful drawing or colouring.

Further development

Posters can, and often do, serve a dual purpose. They can, for instance, both present information and persuade people into action. A poster advertising a competition or award for the 'Most suitably dressed person or class' to be judged on a particular date would be an example of this. The heading may be similar to that of the information poster, for example 'Competition' or 'Are you the best dressed class?', as will the text that gives information about dates and judging criteria. However, the main body of the text will be persuasive in nature (for example, 'Wouldn't *you* like to win...' or 'Imagine yourself winning...').

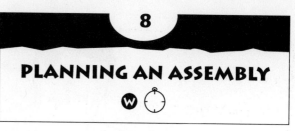
Teaching content

Writing helps to organise thoughts and actions and to remind people of what they have done.

What you need

Large sheets of paper, marker pens, access to charts, posters and other outcomes from previous activities, range of materials for making up new items.

What to do

Gather the children together as a class, reminding them that the date of the school assembly is approaching so it is time to plan the presentation. Recap the different things they have done for the weather project and note this on a large sheet of paper.

Explain that as assembly time will be limited (specify ten minutes) the class must agree on:
• which important items should be included and in what order;
• who will take part in the presentation.

Examine the list of activities done, asking the children to propose which items should be included. 'Star' these, then discuss the order. Number items accordingly, then move on to think about presenters. Some children may prefer not to be in the spotlight but will play a full part in the preparations. Write the names of presenters beside the item they will present.

Ask the children to think about the beginning and end of the presentation and list their ideas on a large sheet of paper. They may suggest introducing the subject/assembly with:
• a song;
• a procession arriving on stage carrying posters
• an announcement.

They may want to end the presentation by the compere summing up with:
• a song (same as before or different);
• a presentation of an award;
• details of the display at the school entrance;
• further questions for other classes to investigate.

Discuss all the ideas and help the class to make a decision. Allocate specific jobs to different children.

End the session by using the lists to recap on the decisions made and make a neat class list

PUBLICATION, CELEBRATION AND REVIEW

Teaching content
Celebration and review.

What you need
One piece of work to review, a reviewer, photocopiable page 86, writing materials.

What to do
This activity may be carried out with reference to any of the activity outcomes described in this project. List the outcomes:
- advertising a competition;
- poster information;
- report on clothing arguments;
- report on 'what did you wear today?'

One reviewer should be the headteacher. The children should choose one piece of work – a report, poster or assembly contribution to present to him or her. It may be something they have written individually, in pairs or as part of a group. The headteacher should be asked to read and discuss this work with small groups, completing one copy of photocopiable page 86 for each piece of work discussed.

Other reviewer(s) might include:
- other children in the class;
- other children in the school;
- a School Governor or School Board member.

The writer, or writers, in question should show the piece of work to the reviewer, explain how and why it was done and what is interesting about it. The reviewer should then be asked to complete a copy of photocopiable page 86.

on large poster paper showing the running order of items, who is involved in each and what they have to do. Discuss whether the children will write their own contributions or whether you will help with this. Arrange a time to meet and rehearse the assembly presentation.

During the rehearsal, ask the children who are not presenting to watch carefully and make constructive comments on how it could be improved. A checklist of 'things to look for' displayed in a prominent place might provide a useful aid to this process.

Prompt the children with the following points if necessary:
- Does the introduction set the scene?
- Could the sequence of items be improved – does one item lead on to the next?
- Do the presenters appear confident, relaxed and knowledgeable?
- Can you easily hear what the presenters say? Do they talk loudly enough? Do they talk too fast? Are they interesting to listen to?
- Is everyone alert? Do they know when to come on to the stage, where to stand and where to go when they have finished?
- Is the ending memorable? Will it make people think?

Scholastic
NON-FICTION WRITING PROJECTS
Workshop

LETTER FROM A HEAD TEACHER

Dear Class _____

On a recent snowy/cold/wet/windy day, I noticed that some children were arriving at school much more suitably dressed for the weather conditions than others. I am interested to know why this is so. I would, for example, like to know if older children dress more or less suitably than younger ones. Do the different age groups prefer different types of weather? What do you think? Also, who decides what children wear to school – is it the children, or their parents or childminders – and do children ever argue about what to wear?

I am looking for a class to investigate these questions and possibly run a campaign to raise everyone's awareness of the importance of dressing to suit the weather conditions. I thought your class might be interested in this task.

I would be happy for you to decide which questions to investigate and how to do this. However, the work might involve:

Background information
• Recording the weather conditions over a period of time to show how changeable the weather actually is.
• Gathering information on the weather preferences of different age groups or classes.

Dressing for the weather
• Carrying out a survey to determine what children in different classes wore to school on a particular day and how appropriate you think this was.
• Interviewing children and their parents about what they wear, why and who decides this.

I would be very interested to read a report of the results of any investigation into these questions and would send a copy to the School Governors/School Board. The work could also be shared with the whole school at an assembly, or a display could be made for the school entrance.

A campaign to encourage everyone to dress suitably for the weather might involve making posters or running a competition to find the best dressed class. You would, of course, be free to decide on this.

I would like you to think about my questions and what you could do to answer any of them. I look forward to hearing from you.

Yours sincerely,

WEATHER RECORD

Names: _____ and _____

The symbols used in
this Weather Record:

| | sun | rain | wind | snow | thunder | lightning |

	Monday	Tuesday	Wednesday	Thursday	Friday	Saturday	Sunday
Week 1	Sun	rain	Sun	Snow	thunder Snow	Snow wind	
Week 2	Light thunder ning	thunder rain	sun	sun	sun Sun	Sun Sun	rain
Week 3	Sun Sun	sun rain	Sun rain	rain Snow	Snow Snow	Snow Snow	Snow Snow

In the past three weeks, the weather has been mostly _Sun_

rain , _Sun_ and _Sun_ with some _____ periods.

WEATHER PREFERENCES

Draw a face to indicate what you think of each type of weather. Choose from the ones below.

Yipadee doo dah!   Oh no, yuk!   No opinion

Quite pleasant   A bit depressing   Worried

Type of weather	My reaction	Type of weather	My reaction

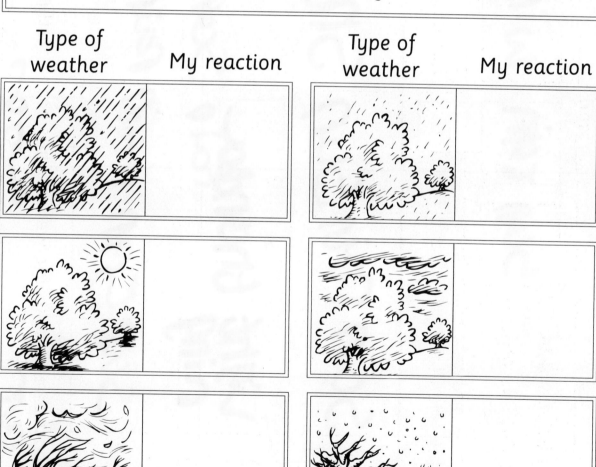

WHAT DID YOU WEAR TODAY?

Survey by _____ Survey of class _____

Total number of children in class: _____

Today the weather is _____

The ideal clothing for today's weather is:

CLOTHING ARGUMENTS: WHO DECIDES?

One thing that surprised me about the reports in this book was _____

_____

_____

The age group that seems to have the most arguments is

_____

_____

_____

The weather that seems to cause the most arguments is

_____

_____

_____

NAME

PUBLICATION, CELEBRATION AND REVIEW

Name of writer:_____

Name of reviewer: _____

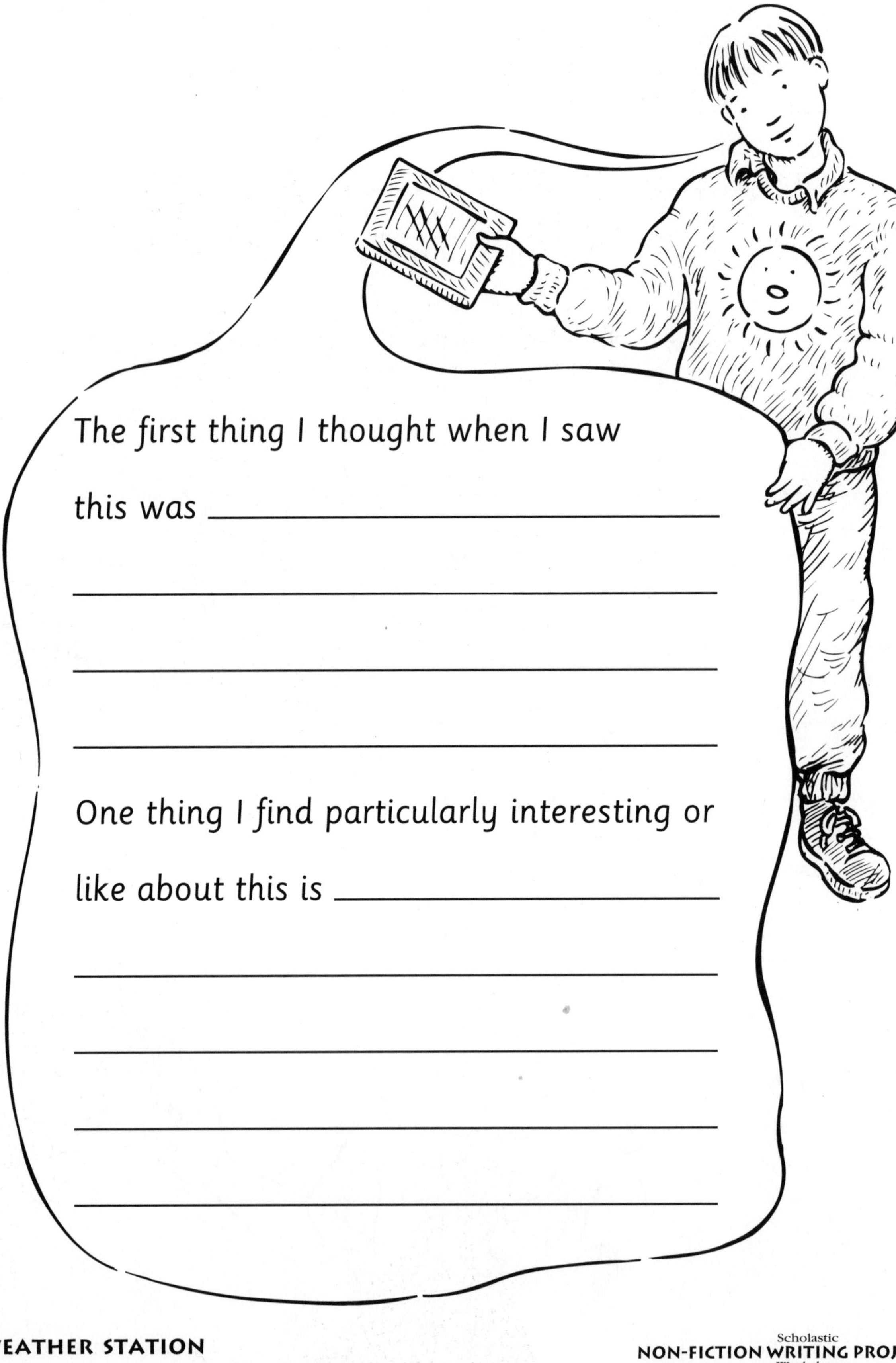

The first thing I thought when I saw

this was _____

_____

_____

_____

One thing I find particularly interesting or

like about this is _____

_____

_____

_____

_____

Scholastic
NON-FICTION WRITING PROJECTS
Workshop

Scholastic WORKSHOP

Chapter Seven

DINOSAUR MUSEUM

INTRODUCTION

Project description

The starting point for this project may be part of a larger topic on dinosaurs, or may result from a visit to a museum or from looking at leaflets about dinosaurs or other types of museums.

During the project the children develop awareness of different genres of functional writing. In setting up a 'Dinosaur Museum' in their classroom they are involved in listing information, identifying different types of writing, designing a survey, creating a variety of information books and writing instructions about how to make dinosaurs. With this background experience children plan the layout and relevant notices, signs and directions needed to complete their museum. The project culminates in another class coming to visit the Dinosaur Museum and both classes evaluating its success.

Why this context?

This project identifies an audience and purpose at the outset. Young children are intrigued by dinosaurs. They are fascinated by their size and have fun in pronouncing the different names. The project provides opportunities for children to practise giving instructions, persuading and giving information using a variety of publishing formats. It offers structure through relevant writing frames to support children in the process. The 'museum' is a suitable context because it gives children a sense of history and may enable them to grasp the concept of 'thousands of years ago'. Children may already have visited museums; however, it may be a good idea to visit a museum if children have not experienced one before. The 'Dinosaur Museum' is being established for another class to visit and the project seeks to involve all children in making this happen.

Project organisation

If this project is free-standing, it will probably take about two weeks to complete. Create a 'dinosaur' area within the classroom large enough to display models of the dinosaurs and background information to support children's writing – leaflets, a variety of dinosaur non-fiction books and a wall display. The project offers a variety of opportunities for both independent and collaborative writing. Class, paired, individual and small-group activities are offered. It will be necessary to arrange a time for another class to come to visit the Dinosaur Museum; and the co-operation of the visiting class's teacher will be needed to help with the survey.

Publication, celebration and review

All writing which is developed through the project is on display when the class visits the Dinosaur Museum. Some materials may be photocopied for children to take away. As well as a display and the Dinosaur Museum table-top plan, children wear badges which give information about their jobs in the museum. The invited class are asked to evaluate their visit and leave their comments for the children to read. The class are also asked to review the aspects of writing which they enjoyed most/least during the project.

Books the children may find useful

Incredible Dinosaurs, Christopher Maynard (1993) Kingfisher Books
Dinosaurs, Angela Royston (1991) Dorling Kindersley
Dinosaurs, Rachel Wright and David Lambert (1993) Franklin Watts
My First Dinosaur Activity Book, Claire Henley (1991) Hippo Books
Dinosaurs, Constance Milburn (1989) Picture Puffin

Set the context for this project by telling the children that over the next week or so they will be discussing museums. To gauge their experiences, ask if any of them have ever been to a museum.

For the first session ask the children to think about what they saw or might see in a museum; what they found out or might find out in a museum, and the types of writing they saw or might see there.

If children have any leaflets about museums at home, ask them to bring these into school. Tell them not to worry if they cannot find any because you will be bringing some in.

1

WHAT DO WE KNOW ABOUT MUSEUMS?

Teaching content

Modelling a list of different types of information. Developing an awareness of instructional and informational genres of writing.

What you need

Large sheet of paper (labelled 'What we know about a museum', 'Types', 'What you see', 'Display', 'Find out about', 'Do/can't do'), a variety of museum leaflets including ones about natural history or dinosaurs if possible, A4 paper, photocopiable page 99, labelled sheet of paper with the headings 'Types of writing' and 'Tells us', writing materials.

What to do

Begin by taking feedback from the children. Remind them that you asked them to think about museums. Brainstorm the children for suggestions about what they know about museums. Ask them what types of museum they have visited or would like to visit, for example a toy museum, a science museum, and so on. Record the children's ideas on the first large sheet of paper under the heading 'Types'. Then ask what kinds of things can be seen in a museum. How are the various objects displayed? For example, exhibits may be hung on the wall, there may be models or objects in glass cases. Again, record the children's answers under the appropriate headings.

Ask what you would find out in a museum. This might include where the objects come from, what they are made of and any special features. Again, record all of the children's ideas on the large sheet of paper. Tell them that they have given a lot of information, and ask how a museum gives the visitor information. The children may suggest labels, leaflets, guidebooks and notices.

Finally ask what people can and cannot do in a museum, for example 'look', 'not touch', 'find out', 'read about', 'not run'. Add these to the sheet and attach it to the wall for the children to refer to.

Next organise the children into groups of four. Hand out some paper and the leaflets that you, and they, have brought in. Using the information recorded on the large sheet of paper and in the leaflets, ask the children to write down the different types of writing they may see in a museum and what they might tell us about or tell us to do. For example:

• Signs tell us which way to go.
• Notices tell us to do or not to do something.
• Labels tell us about the exhibits.
• A noticeboard displays details of special events and opening times.
• A map or a plan tells us where things are located.

When the children have had enough time to list three or four types of writing and their purposes, take a suggestion from one of the groups and record it on the large sheet of paper labelled 'Types of writing' and 'Tells us'. Go round each group until all ideas have been suggested or you have a sufficient number on the list (retain this sheet for use in a later session).

Tell the children that they will be using much of this information to help them create a Dinosaur Museum in the classroom. At the end of the project they will invite another class in to see it.

Conclude the session by asking the children to think about three things they already know about one type of dinosaur, for example its name, what it looked like and one other thing,

such as what it ate. Children may be able to do this without reference books. You may, however, want to let children borrow books about dinosaurs to take home or allow some time in the class for them to consult information books.

Cut out the dinosaur strips on photocopiable page 99 and give one strip to each child. Explain that they should take these home, write the name of the dinosaur, draw and/or write what it looks like and write down anything else they know about their dinosaur on the dinosaur strip.

Ask them to bring the strips back for the next session.

WHAT DO WE KNOW ABOUT DINOSAURS?

Teaching content
Creating a table to give information and considering audience by thinking about questions to ask another class.

What you need
Completed dinosaur strips from Session 1, a dinosaur strip which the teacher has completed, large sheets of paper, adhesive.

What to do
Gather the class together, asking them to bring their dinosaur strips with them, and begin this session by showing the children the dinosaur strip that *you* have completed. Read through the different sections with the children.

The organisation of the next part of this session will largely depend on which dinosaurs have been selected. Ask the children to put up their hands if they have written about Tyrannosaurus Rex. Allocate a table or tables for them to sit at. Repeat this for the other dinosaurs that have been written about. Group sizes will obviously vary. Give each group a large sheet of paper (some may need two sheets depending on how big their group is) and tell the children to stick their dinosaur strips one under the other to create a table of information.

Finally tell the children that as another class will be visiting their Dinosaur Museum it would

be useful to know what *they* would like to find out about dinosaurs. For the next session, ask the children to think of questions they could put to the visiting class in order to find out what they want to know.

SURVEY TIME

Teaching content
A survey helps us to find things out. In a survey we need to ask a lot of people the same questions. We can record how many people gave the same answer by tallying.

What you need
Large sheets of paper, marker pens, A4 paper, examples of questionnaires and survey forms, photocopiable page 100 (enlarged to A3 if necessary), writing materials.

What to do
Note: Before this session begins, remind the visiting class's teacher that a small group from your class will be coming in to undertake the survey.

At the end of the previous session, children were asked to think of questions they could ask another class in order to discover what they would like to find out about dinosaurs. Gather the class together and ask the children for their questions. Be responsive to the various questions, some of which may not be suitable for a survey. Record the main points on a large sheet of paper, for example size, type of food dinosaurs ate, size or type of teeth, and so on. Explain to the children that the best way to find out what the other class would like to know would be by carrying out a survey in which they could ascertain exactly what aspects of dinosaurs the other class would like to know more about. Decide on the main categories for the survey and a heading such as 'What would you like to know about dinosaurs?'

Talk about the format for this survey. Explain that there are various ways of carrying out a survey. Some may ask for a simple 'Yes' or 'No' answer. In others we may vote for a choice, while in some surveys we may give answers to open-ended questions. If you have managed to obtain any examples of questionnaires or

surveys, show these to the children along with your copy of photocopiable page 100 which illustrates some of the various ways in which information in surveys can be obtained.

Ask the children how they could make their survey simple to fill in. Will it ask children in the visiting class to reply 'Yes' or 'No' to various questions? Will they tick a box if they want to know about size, for instance? Will there be signs or symbols on the survey form? Will there be blank boxes for children to fill in if they want to find out any other information?

Remind the children of the main categories they decided upon. Organise the children into small groups (children can work in different groups from the previous sessions if you or they wish) and give each group a sheet of A4 paper. Ask them to design a simple survey sheet. Suggest possible formats to help the children get started, such as boxes with one heading in each which the children completing the survey can tick if they would like information. Figure 1 shows an example.

Do you want to know about...	
size	
teeth	
food	

Figure 1

Remind the children to keep in their minds a picture of who their survey is for and what they are trying to find out from it.

Give the children time to complete this then bring the class back together and ask the groups to talk about the purpose of their survey. Select one of the designs. Explain that four children will be visiting the other class to conduct the survey, so you will be making four copies of this design. Display the other surveys on the wall so that the children feel they have contributed and that their work has been valued.

Choose four children to conduct the survey and send them to the other class to carry it out. Each child should be allocated one group from which to gather the information. How the responses are recorded will vary according to the design of the survey but one option would be for the children to record the responses in the form of a tally mark. On their return, work with the four children who conducted the survey to collate their responses. Identify three or four of the most popular aspects of dinosaurs that the children in the visiting class would like to know about. These will form the basis of writing activities in the next session. Feed back the results to the rest of the class.

DINO INFO.

Teaching content
Information can be written in reports which may vary in presentation.

What you need
Writing and drawing materials, card, stapler, a selection of non-fiction books including dinosaur reference books, photocopiable pages 101 and 102, scissors, paper fasteners, adhesive, A4 paper, A5 paper, paper slightly larger than A4, card for labels.

What to do
This session builds on the information obtained in the previous session and provides children with the opportunity to work in pairs to make books for the Dinosaur Museum. It may be most easily managed with a different group working on their book each day. Explain to the children that four different book formats will be created and what they will all have in common is the information they will contain. The selection of information will be guided by the results of the survey, in which the children from the other class highlighted the information they would like to know about dinosaurs. Children need to turn the statements in the survey into questions and answers for the books. Organise the children into four groups.

Group One
Tell the children in this group that they will be working in pairs to create a simple A4 sized 'All About...' book. Explain that it will be a question and answer book and will require three pages (one page for each question and answer) and a front cover. These will then all be stapled at the side to create a book.

Explain that the children will need to decide:
• which dinosaur to write about;
• which question to write on each page;
• what to write in response to the questions.

Spend time with each pair looking at the way in which information is displayed in non-fiction books. Explore how layout, labels, diagrams and pictures all contribute to the overall presentation.

Choose one of the reference books on dinosaurs and discuss particular features of the

Figure 2

Figure 3

The children should then cut out the wheel on photocopiable page 102 and place it behind the cut out shape. Attach the wheel with a paper fastener to the back cover. See Figure 5.

Tell the children to paste the two corners of their pages shut. See Figure 6

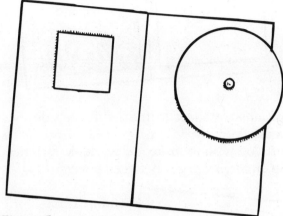

Figure 5

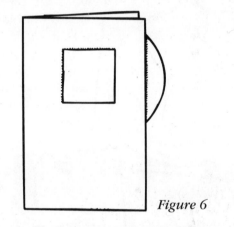

Figure 6

book: relevant facts given on different pages, questions, different sizes of print, writing arranged in different ways (for example around the pictures). When you feel the children have a suitable understanding, offer them suggestions for the structure of their book. Figures 2 and 3 show an example of what the front cover and one of the pages could look like.

Children may wish to make a draft copy before creating the final version of their book. The activity may therefore last a few days as part of on-going class work or work on the project.

Next they can illustrate the front cover. See Figure 7.

They then draw pictures on the wheel, turning the wheel until pictures have been drawn all around it. See Figure 8.

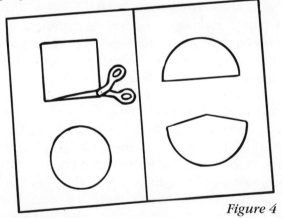

Figure 4

The children paste the wheel page on to the right-hand side of a sheet of paper,

Figure 7

Group Two

Organise children into pairs to create a wheel book. Give each pair a copy of photocopiable pages 101 and 102. Tell them to cut all around the dotted outline of page 101. They should then choose one of the shapes on the sheet, cut it out then fold the page in half across the fold line. See Figure 4.

slightly larger than A4. They can then attach a question

Figure 8

Figure 9

and answer sheet to the left-hand side. See Figure 9.

If you wish to make a class book, fasten all the children's pages between covers.

Figure 10

inside back cover. See Figure 10. Give the children a sheet of A5 paper and ask them to copy the

Figure 11

bottom half of their illustration. See Figure 11. The children write their questions and answers on separate sheets of A5 paper. These sheets and the bottom half of the illustration are then stapled together at the side to create the final version. The children should write the title and their names on the front as in Figure 12.

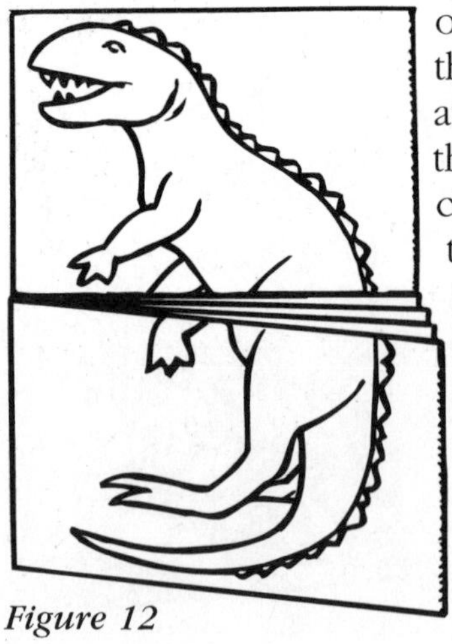

Figure 12

Group Three

The third group will work in pairs to create a Book-and-a-Half.

To make this the children first draw an illustration on a sheet of A4 paper. This forms the

Group Four

With this group, introduce the children to the idea of a caption or

noticeboard that can be placed beside the dinosaurs which they will make or bring into school. On a sheet of folded card children should write three or four different labels giving different pieces of information about their dinosaur, with a picture in the centre. Figure 13 shows an example.

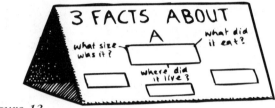

Figure 13

When all the groups have completed their various displays ask them to show them to the rest of the class. Explain that the various book formats will be displayed when the visiting class comes to the Dinosaur Museum.

BRING ON THE DINOSAURS
W → † 60

Teaching content

When writing instructions we need to give a title, what is needed and numbered steps to follow a process. We use action words.

What you need

A4 paper, writing and drawing materials, an enlarged copy of photocopiable page 103 for demonstration with the class, photocopiable page 104, dinosaur reference books.

What to do

Recap with the children the work they have done so far. They have carried out a survey and have created various information books – but there are no dinosaurs to put in the Dinosaur Museum. Ask the children if they have any toy dinosaurs at home which they would be willing to bring in. Remind them to ask permission from their families. However, they will still need a lot of dinosaurs for display.

Explain that half of the class are going to choose a dinosaur each, and then draw it on a sheet of A4. Allow them to look through the dinosaur reference books if they need ideas. Start this group off and explain to the rest of the class that their task will be to make individual dinosaurs using modelling materials. These can be clay, Plasticine or play dough, depending on what is available in your classroom. Again, allow them to consult the reference books if they need inspiration or fresh ideas.

When the children have completed their tasks, gather the class together. Compliment them on their dinosaurs, and tell them that you now want them to design a sheet which will give the visiting class instructions about how *they* could make or draw a dinosaur.

Show the children your enlarged copy of photocopiable page 103 and draw their attention to the action words used – 'see', 'add', 'draw', and so on. Explain that following instructions, in order, leads to a finished product.

Hand out copies of photocopiable page 104 and explain that it provides a writing frame in which the children will write instructions for how to draw or make their dinosaur. Point out that there is a space to complete a title, for instance 'How to draw a Diplodocus' or 'How to make a Stegosaurus'. They should complete the title with the name of their chosen dinosaur, list what materials are needed to draw or make the dinosaur and then describe the steps. Each step should begin with an action word such as 'add', 'draw', 'put'. You may have to support this part of the activity by prompting the children with questions such as 'What did you draw/make first? What did you do next? Finally?'

Tell the children that their completed photocopiable sheets will also be displayed in the Dinosaur Museum. The 'How to draw a dinosaur' sheets can be displayed on a frieze beside the children's drawings. The 'How to

make a dinosaur' sheets can be displayed beside one or two dinosaurs, with the others kept in a box for the visiting class to look at or take away.

WHAT GOES WHERE?

Teaching content

Rules tell people what to do or not to do. Directions need to be simple and concise, using words like 'forward', 'left', 'right', 'next to', 'start at'. Signs and notices provide clear information in words, pictures or symbols.

What you need

Large sheet of paper labelled 'We have', 'We need', sheet from Session 1 labelled 'Types of writing' and 'Tells us', marker pens, an area in the classroom with card or paper large enough to cover this area, tables, large paper, photocopiable page 105, writing, drawing and painting materials.

What to do

Using the labelled sheet of paper, begin by reviewing what has been done and what still needs to be done for the museum. Under the heading 'We have' can be written: responses to surveys, different types of information books, toy dinosaurs, drawings and models of dinosaurs, 'how to draw' and 'how to make'

instruction sheets. Remind the children of the sheet that was collated in the first session which listed the types of writing found in a museum. Ask them to suggest what still needs to be done in order to make part of the classroom into a museum. Suggestions should include:

• deciding where exactly in the classroom the museum will be located;

• various notices and signs giving information about the exhibits;

• a list of rules;

• a list of directions.

Record the ideas on the large sheet under the heading 'We need'. Show the children the area set aside for the museum. The allocation of space will largely depend on the size of your classroom. (You may or may not have set out tables at this point.) Explain that you will be working with a small group to make a plan of the museum and create a small-world play area. In pairs, the other children will create a list of rules, directions and signs/notices/labels that they feel are necessary for the museum. Give each pair a copy of photocopiable page 105 on which to draft their ideas. (You may need a class assistant to help with the organisation of this session.)

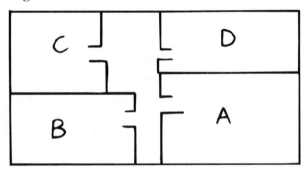

Figure 14

With the small group, use the card or paper to cover the tables in the museum area. On a separate piece of paper draw a simple plan of the Dinosaur Museum, identifying different 'rooms' in which the various types of dinosaurs will be exhibited. Figure 14 gives an example of how the plan may look.

Draw this in pencil at the moment. Next ask the group to decide which exhibits will go in the different 'rooms'. Ask them to record this on a separate sheet of paper. As they are doing this, draw a copy of the plan on large paper to use with the whole class later. This floor plan can be painted by the children at a later point in the session.

Gather the class back together and show everyone the floor plan for the museum. Take feedback from the children who have been creating the rules, directions and signs, listing their ideas on a large sheet of paper.

Rules

Begin with their suggestions for rules. These may include:

• Be quiet.

• Don't touch.

• Don't steal.

• Don't drop litter.

Explain to the children that rules are often written as commands.

Decide with the children which rules should be used in the museum and allocate two or three children to write these on card. On a separate piece of card write a heading for these rules, such as 'When you visit our museum'. The rules can then be added to the small world play area.

Directions

Now that the floor plan has been drawn, the children will be able to add appropriate directions or design a key to the layout of the museum. Allocate some children to write the directions on strips of paper or card. Another group can make a mini-floor plan, using your original plan, to give to the visiting class.

Signs, notices, labels

Tell the children that the main sign will probably say something such as 'The Dinosaur Museum'. A small group or pair of children can paint or draw this in suitable lettering for the area. Other children should be given the task of creating any signs or notices which either remain unassigned on the list brainstormed at the beginning of the session or that they have subsequently thought of. A group may now paint in the floor plan. All children should have a task to do. When all the tasks are completed set the items and dinosaur exhibits in place.

PEOPLE IN THE MUSEUM

w → (60)

Teaching content

Descriptions help to give us information about the jobs people do.

What you need

A3 paper for posters, card cut into circles for badges, drawing pins or ribbons for badges, large sheet of paper, writing and drawing materials.

What to do

Begin this session by reminding children that the Dinosaur Museum has now been set up. The dinosaurs are in place and there are signs, directions and information books. However, there are no people to help in the museum.

Brainstorm with the children the different kinds of jobs there are in a museum. Write these on a large sheet of paper. Then, using a different coloured pen, write underneath what the job might involve. For example:

a guide	shows people around
an information officer	hands out leaflets and books
a security guard	makes sure you don't touch or steal
a tea room	serves hot and cold drinks
a photographer	provides a memento of your visit
an expert	stands at the displays to explain the exhibits
a nurse	is on stand-by in case anyone faints or becomes ill.

Ask the children what job they would like to do on the day the visiting class comes to see their museum. Organise the children accordingly, ensuring that there are more or less equal numbers at each job.

When this has been completed, each child should make a badge with a picture of her or himself and the title of his or her job. They will wear these on the day that the other class visits.

COME TO THE DINOSAUR MUSEUM

w → (60)

Teaching content

Designing a poster/leaflet to give information.

What you need

A letter from the visiting class, A3 paper, photocopiable page 106, a variety of museum leaflets (as used in Session 1), writing and drawing materials.

What to do

Prior to this session you will need to arrange for the visiting class to write a letter to your class. The letter should request information about:

• what time to come;
• where to find the museum;
• whether there is an entrance fee;
• what they will see at the museum.

Arrange for a messenger to deliver this letter to your class at the beginning of the session. Read the letter to the class and ask whether they would like to reply, giving answers to the information requested.

Remind them that at the beginning of the project they looked at different leaflets about museums. Suggest that a leaflet may be a good way to give the visiting class the information they require. Similarly, some children may want to design a poster. Ask children to choose one format (poster or leaflet) and then organise them into pairs. Show them photocopiable page 106 and look at the sheet with them. Explain that they can use this to gather information and do a draft layout before they design their leaflets or posters.

Explain that whether they make a leaflet or a poster, they need to think about:
• the reason for the leaflet or poster– to give information;
• the audience – who will read it;
• what information the visiting class have requested – content;
• how this should be organised and displayed – layout.

Tell the children the day you have selected for the other class to visit. Give each pair a copy of photocopiable page 106 and set them to work. As in Session 1 allow the children to refer to the published leaflets for ideas, but remind them of the main features of their 'own' museum.

When the children have finished, gather the class together and compose a letter to the visiting class to accompany the package of leaflets and posters. For example:

Dear Class _____,

We have made some posters and leaflets to give you information about our Dinosaur Museum. We hope that you will come.

From Class _____.

9

CELEBRATION AND REVIEW

Ⓦ 60

Teaching content
Evaluating the writing aspects of the project which children enjoyed most/least.

What you need
The Dinosaur Museum and a display of all writing completed by the class during the project, drinks for the visiting class, photocopiable pages 107 and 108, writing materials, ribbon for the opening.

What to do
Before the visiting class arrive, the children should be 'in role' wearing their job badges and with all associated labelling and writing in place.

If you wish, one child can cut an opening ribbon to let the class in and a couple of children could give a speech of welcome. The classroom may be too small to accommodate all the visitors at the same time so it may be preferable for them to come in groups.

Encourage the children to show their visitors around the museum and refer them to the signs, posters, notices, labels and information books on display. If copies of the books made by the class have been made, these can be given to the visiting class.

At the end of the visit, the visiting class should be given copies of photocopiable page 107 and asked to return them to a given point in the museum, perhaps in a special box labelled 'We welcome your comments' or 'Comments here please'.

When the visit is over, congratulate the children on their success and give each child a copy of photocopiable page 108. Ask them to write down which aspects of the project they did or did not enjoy writing about. Share the children's comments with the rest of the class. The Dinosaur Museum should, however, be left for children to use in a free-play situation. They can add new writing about dinosaurs to the museum if they wish.

WHAT DO WE KNOW ABOUT DINOSAURS?

What else do you know?

Looks like

Name

What else do you know?

Looks like

Name

SURVEY TIME

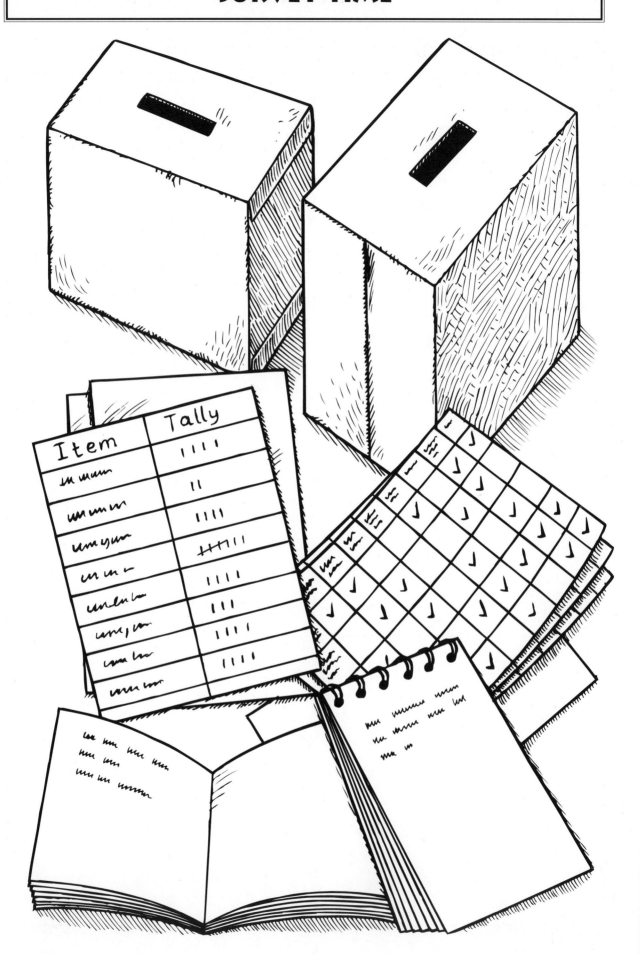

Scholastic
NON-FICTION WRITING PROJECTS
Workshop

WHEEL BOOK

Cut out *one* opening.

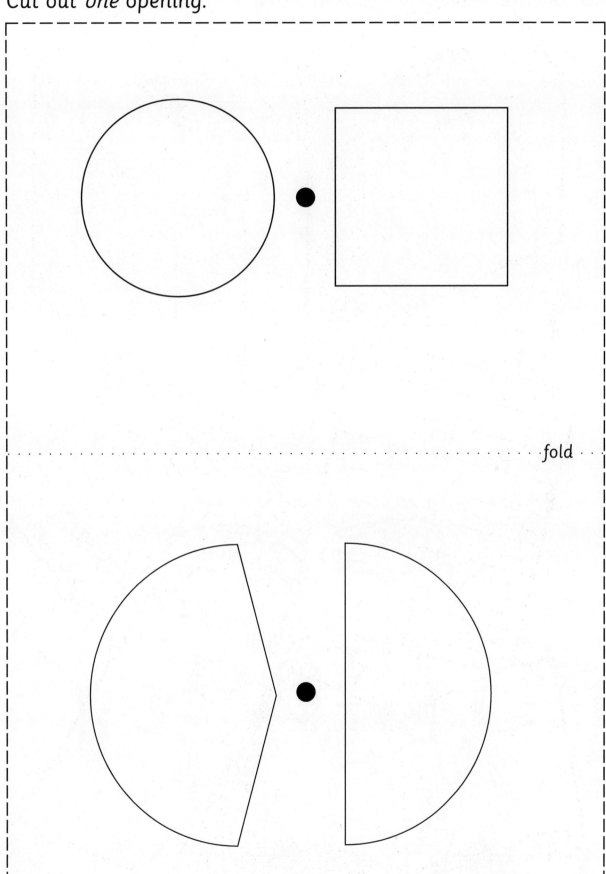

fold

WHEEL BOOK

Cut out the wheel.

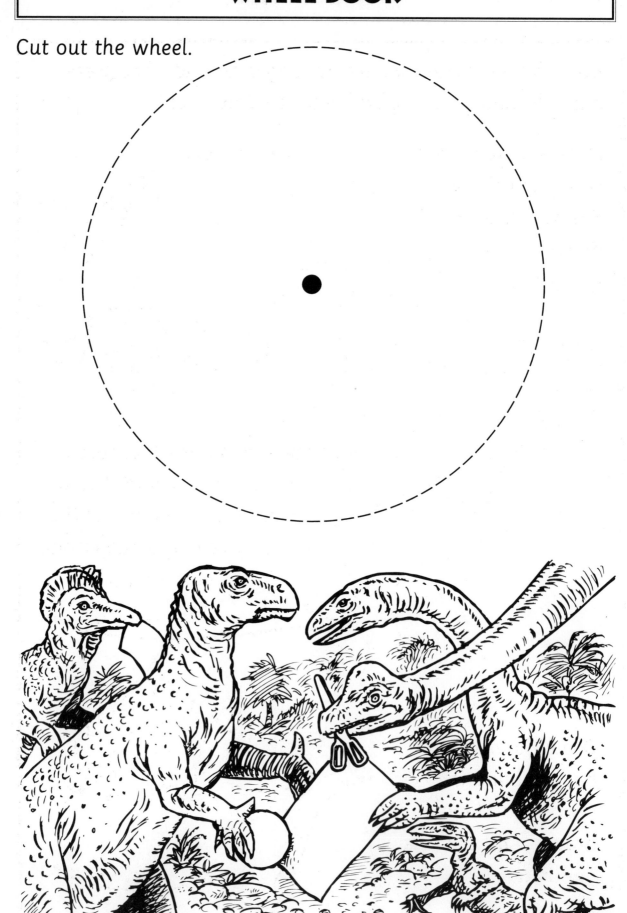

DINOSAURS

Even though dinosaurs are no longer around, they *were* animals, and you may still want to draw one!

Here is a **stegosaurus** seen from the side. See how it is based on a curve for its back.

Brachiosaurus

You can draw a good Brachiosaurus by starting with a curve. Add a small oval at the top of the curve and a bigger one in the centre.

Draw the neck and body around the shapes you have drawn. Add the legs and head.

BRING ON THE DINOSAURS

How to

You will need

This is what you do:

1.

2.

3.

4.

WHAT GOES WHERE?

Rules	Directions

Signs/Notices/Labels

COME TO THE DINOSAUR MUSEUM

Title:

What time?	Where is it?
How much will it cost?	**What is in the museum?**

Draft layout

THANK YOU FOR COMING

Dear Visitor

Thank you for visiting our Dinosaur Museum. Please tell us what you enjoyed and why.

I enjoyed

because

Any other comments

Thank you for your comments.

CELEBRATION AND REVIEW

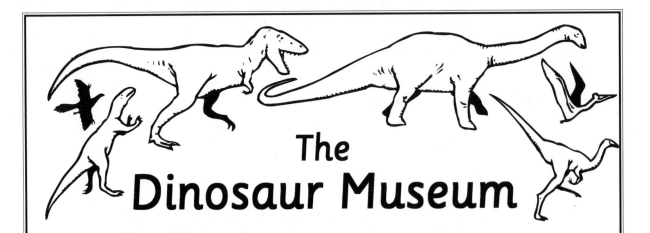

The Dinosaur Museum

Dear

Thank you for all your hard work to create a Dinosaur Museum. I would like to know:

Which writing did you enjoy most?

Why?

Which writing did you not enjoy?

Why?

What should we do now with our Dinosaur Museum?

Scholastic WORKSHOP

Chapter Eight

MEMORIES

INTRODUCTION

Project description

In this project the children compile a timeline of memories. They begin by creating a class diary – recording what they did at the weekend and on the previous day. They move on to look back at their memories of their first day at school, at their favourite toys and activities as toddlers and babies, and their parents, or relatives, first memories of them. Delving further into the past they research changes over time, particularly in schools. Visitors are invited into school and asked about their memories of the past. The children then record and display these memories. Parents, grandparents or older members of the community can be invited to view the displays.

Why this context?

It is valuable for children's learning to encourage them to look back on experiences they have had, to share these memories with others and to review and evaluate their experiences. Creating a 'shared history' within the classroom or school provides opportunities to explore individual similarities and differences and gives each child the chance to view their experience in class, school, family and community settings as unique and valued. In exploring the immediate and more distant past the children will gain some understanding of the passage of time, and changes over time, in a context which is meaningful to them.

Children's functional writing skills are developed naturally as they recount past experiences and collect, record and display the memories of others. The children design questionnaires, plan and conduct interviews, and research and record facts from functional texts. The class timeline will display all the information for others to see. This can be shared by inviting visitors to see the timeline and having the children explain it, or the children could make a video-recording of their classmates explaining each aspect of the timeline.

Project organisation

This project provides opportunities for individual, group and whole-class work. Individual work involves the children in personal research into their own past and recounting and recording this information. Collaborative group work involves decision making, collating and displaying information for others to learn from. Opportunities for class work include looking back at the children's own experiences, making decisions about suitable ways to collect and display information and interviewing members of the community about changes and their memories. Parents and grandparents or older members of the community are necessary and ideal sources of information for the success of this project and children are expected to bring information and possibly photographs and artefacts from home. In one session adults are invited into the class to be interviewed by the children.

Publication, celebration and review

Each session produces an end product which becomes part of the timeline. The display of the timeline is the publication. The children's work is celebrated by them recognising in Session 8 how they have changed and developed. The celebration can be shared either by the children presenting a school assembly or inviting older friends and relatives into school for an explanation of the timeline. If a video camera is available the children can present their timeline information by making a video recording as suggested in Session 9.

Books the children may find useful

Starting History Series, *Our schools,* (1994), *Our family,* (1992) and *Where we lived,* (1994) Stewart Ross, Wayland

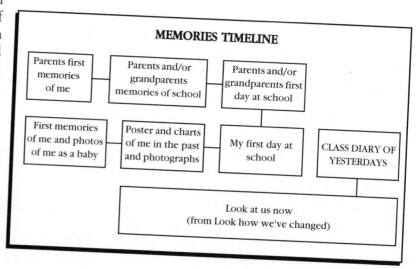

MEMORIES TIMELINE

Parents first memories of me	Parents and/or grandparents memories of school	Parents and/or grandparents first day at school
First memories of me and photos of me as a baby	Poster and charts of me in the past and photographs	My first day at school · CLASS DIARY OF YESTERDAYS

Look at us now
(from Look how we've changed)

WHAT DID YOU DO AT THE WEEKEND?

Teaching content
We can recall what we did at the weekend and write it in simple past tense.

What you need
A3 sheets of paper labelled 'At the weekend' (one for each group), A4 sheets of paper cut into quarters, writing and drawing materials, adhesive, large sheets of paper, marker pens.

What to do
Bring the class together and tell them that you had a busy weekend. Say, for example, 'At the weekend I went shopping for a new coat, watched a film at the cinema and went for a walk in the park with my family'. Ask the children what they did at the weekend and say they should begin their answer with 'At the weekend...'. Take a few of their answers and repeat them. Draw the children's attention to the 'doing' words and ask if they notice anything about them, for example 'went', 'walked', 'watched', 'saw', 'visited', 'drove'. You may like to write these on a large sheet of paper for the children to refer to.

Explain that because these things happened in the past – yesterday or the day before – we use words that describe the past:
- not go but went;
- not watch but watched;
- not walk but walked;
- not see but saw;
- not visit but visited;
- not drive but drove.

Ask a few more children to tell everyone what they did at the weekend and as they answer draw their attention to the past tense verbs or phrases that they use.

Tell the children that they are going to make a class diary of their week. The first page will begin with 'At the weekend...'. Show them the quartered sheets of paper and explain that they have to draw a picture and write about *one* thing they did at the weekend. For example, if John went skating he would write 'I went skating'. If Ayshah watched cartoons on TV she would write 'I watched cartoons on TV'. Organise the children into groups and issue

one piece of paper to each child. Encourage the children to write their own sentence but help those who need it by suggesting vocabulary or scribing for them. Appoint one child to be a group leader and give this child an A3 sheet of paper labelled 'At the weekend...'.

When each child has completed their story and picture tell them to paste it on to the A3 group sheet, ensuring they leave enough space for everyone's picture and story.

This session provides the first few pages of the class diary.

YESTERDAY

Teaching content
What the class did on the previous day can be recorded in simple past tense.

What you need
A3 sheet of paper labelled 'Yesterday' with the correct day and date written after the word 'Yesterday', A4 paper cut into quarters, writing and drawing materials, adhesive, chalkboard.

What to do
In this session the children compile a recount of what their class did on the previous day. This forms the next page of the class diary. The previous session provides a model for the

children to follow. (Depending on the organisation of your class you may find it most useful to carry out this session with one group at a time. One group writing a page for each day of the week would be best.)

Explain to the children that they are going to create another page for the class diary by recalling what their class did on the previous day and writing about it.

Ask the children if they can remember what their class did on the previous day. In answering they should say 'Yesterday our class...'. Take a different suggestion from each child and write any difficult vocabulary on the board. Draw the children's attention again to the use of the past tense for the verbs, for example:

- had gym;
- did maths;
- sang with the music teacher.

Give each child a quartered sheet of paper. Explain that, as in the previous session, they have to draw a picture and write one sentence about what their class did on the previous day. Their sentence will begin 'Our class...'. These should be stuck on to the A3 sheets headed 'Yesterday' when completed. These sheets are then added to the sheets from Session 1 and the diary grows.

When the children have finished, one group should design and make a cover for the front and back of 'Our Class Diary'. Staple the pages

of the diary together and ask each child who contributed to sign the back cover.

The diary is then hung on the wall as the first (or last) item on the timeline.

Tell the children that in the next session they will be remembering their first day at school. Ask them to talk to their family and to seek their parents' permission to bring in any photographs taken on that day.

MY FIRST DAY AT SCHOOL

Teaching content
Memories of how we felt and what we remember can be written in the simple past tense.

What you need
Chalkboard, photocopiable page 118, photographs of children's first day at school, writing and drawing materials.

What to do
Ask the children who have brought in photographs taken on their first day at school if you can borrow them for the duration of the lesson. Also display any photographs the school may have of the children's first day at school. Gather the children around and focus their attention on the photographs. Ask questions to encourage the children to think more deeply about what they see:

- Who do you think this is?
- What is he or she wearing?
- Does he or she look happy, sad, worried, pleased?

Explore their first day at school:

- How did they feel?
- What did they like?
- What did they not like?
- Who was their teacher?
- Can they remember what he or she was like?
- What did they do?
- Who brought them to school and collected them?
- Was their mum, dad, gran, childminder happy, sad, worried, pleased?
- Did they miss them?

As the children give their answers write some of the important words on the board for them to refer to later.

Show the children a copy of photocopiable page 118. Explain that they must complete the sentences in the boxes and then draw pictures to match what they have written. Remind them that some of the words they may need to complete it are on the board. Issue each child with a photocopiable sheet and help those who need it by suggesting vocabulary or scribing for them.

Some of the completed photocopiable sheets, and the photographs which the children have brought in, should be used to make a collage for the next time slot on the timeline. The remaining photocopiable sheets can be collated into a book and hung beside the collage or kept in project folders.

An interesting extension to this session would be for the children to take home uncompleted copies of photocopiable page 118 and ask their mum, dad, gran or grandpa to complete them, thus compiling memories of another generation's first day at school. These could also be added to the timeline.

4

MEMORIES OF SCHOOL PAST

Teaching content
We can find things out by writing questions for people to answer.

What you need
Reference and information books on schools (particularly those that have pictures and text about schools in the past), photocopiable page 119, writing materials, scrap paper.

What to do
Remind the children of the work they did in the previous session, in which they talked and wrote about their memories of their first day at school. Tell them that everyone they know, whatever age they are, will have some memories of their school days. Ask the children how they could find out about these interesting memories of schools in the past.

Hopefully, the children will suggest that they could ask questions or read books. Explain that you have some books which give information about schools in the past and you are going to read and show them some extracts. Ask the

children what they would like to find out about. Tell them that as they listen, you want them to try to remember the different things the pages tell them about.

Read the books, stopping at appropriate points to draw the children's attention to things they may find interesting, for example assemblies, furniture, the work, the teachers, playtime, PE, and so on.

When you have finished reading, explain to the children that they are going to work in groups to compile a list of four or five things they would like to find out about schools in the past. (You may like to make these groups mixed ability so that the children can support each other.) Appoint one child in each group to be the scribe and hand out some scrap paper. Stress that it is the ideas that are important so they should not worry too much if they cannot spell certain words.

When each group has completed their list of items, check what they have written and issue a copy of photocopiable page 119 to each group. Discuss the sheet with the class, explaining that in the next session each group will be having a visitor who will talk about his or her school days and answer questions from the children. Tell the children that they will use the photocopiable sheet to prepare the questions they would like to ask.

Explain to the children that you would like them to write the item they have highlighted as wanting to know more about in the left-hand

column. In the middle column they will write questions relating to that subject. For example:

The classroom	What did the classroom look like? Did you sit at desks?
Punishment	What happened to you if you were naughty?
Playtime	What games did you play?
The work	What did you learn about?

In the right-hand column they will record the answers that their visitor gives them.

When each group has completed their photocopiable sheet, make copies so that each child in the group has one to refer to. They should be encouraged to take the sheet home and practise their questions before the next session.

5

TELL US ABOUT YOUR SCHOOL DAYS

Teaching content
You can find out information by asking questions and noting down answers.

What you need
Children's completed copies of photocopiable page 119 (including copies for the visitor), writing materials, one visitor per group – teachers, parents, grandparents, members of the community.

What to do
Remind the class of the work they did in the previous session and the questions they prepared. Explain that each group is going to have one visitor. Tell the children that you would like the group scribe from the previous session to ask the person's name and when he or she went to school and note this on the sheet with the visitor's help. In each group allocate one child to ask one of the questions and to note that answer. Ask the adults if they will note the answers briefly on their sheets and help children if necessary.

Introduce the adult visitors to the children and explain to the children that they have 15 minutes to find out their information and note it down. Be on hand to monitor each group's progress and to give help and support where required.

When the groups have finished, thank the visitors and collect their completed photocopiable sheets.

Each group should then take 5 minutes to read through their information, ensuring that it is clear and they understand it, before presenting it orally to the other groups under the heading 'What we learned about schools in the past'. The sheets completed by the adults should be displayed at the appropriate place on the timeline. Some children may like to illustrate these.

6

ME IN THE PAST

Teaching content
You can give and find information in pictures and charts.

What you need
Enlarged copy of photocopiable page 120 for demonstration with the class, photocopiable page 121, writing and drawing materials.

What to do

Bring the children together as a class. Focus their attention on the timeline they have created and remind them of the last thing they recorded about their own past – their first day at school. Ask the children if they can remember anything about their lives before they went to school – perhaps when they were four or when they were toddlers or even babies. Some children may have memories or knowledge based on what other people have told them.

Introduce your enlarged copy of photocopiable page 120 and see if the children can 'read' it. Ask questions to encourage understanding. 'What does it tell us about a baby of one? What does a baby of one like to play with? Eat? Wear? What does a baby of one travel in?'

Model the same questions and interpretation of the photocopiable sheet for a toddler aged two or three and an older child aged four or five.

Play a listening and identifying game with the children to check their understanding. For instance, you could say:
• 'Hands up those who can tell me what this four year old likes to play with.'
• 'Hands up those who can tell me what this baby wears.'
• 'What age is the child who likes fish fingers?'
• 'Whose favourite clothes are dungarees?'

Ask the children if they can remember some of these things about themselves. 'What was their favourite toy when they were a baby? Which place did they like to visit when they were five?'

Explain that they are going to fill in a chart like this for themselves. They will probably not be able to remember all the information as some of it relates to a time when they were very young, but you would like them to make a start in school. They will then be able to take the sheet home for a few days and ask their parents to help them complete the sections they cannot remember.

Give each child a copy of photocopiable page 121 and show them how to complete it. Explain that they can either draw or write the information in the boxes.

Suggest that if the children have photographs, toys or clothes at home relating to these stages of their lives they may like to bring them into school.

If articles are brought in, a table can be set aside for their display and the children encouraged to make labels for them. For instance:
• This was my favourite teddy when I was two. John
• My special party dress when I was one. Shazia

These artefacts could be arranged in age-groups in the same way as the poster.

The enlarged copy of photocopiable page 120 could be hung on the timeline with the photographs and some of the children's completed copies of photocopiable page 121 displayed around it. The remaining photocopiable sheets could form a book called 'Me In The Past'.

FIRST MEMORIES OF ME

Teaching content

We can get information from other people, record it and display it for others to gain information.

What you need

A photograph of yourself as a baby, photocopiable page 122, writing and drawing materials.

What to do

Gather the class together and tell them you have something very special to show them.

Show them the photograph of yourself as a baby and ask if they can guess who it might be. At an appropriate point tell them it is a photograph of you when you were a baby. Explain that you cannot remember yourself when you were a baby, what you were like or what you did, but other people can. Share some of these memories with the children. For example, 'My mum said I was always hungry.'

Tell them the age at which you can remember your earliest memory, for example when you were about three or four. Describe what the memory is and expand upon it. You could say something such as 'I remember going on my holidays – it was the first time I went on a boat'.

Ask the children if they can recall their first memory and encourage them in turn to describe it to the rest of the class.

Organise the children into groups. Give each child a copy of photocopiable page 122 and explain that in the bottom frame they should draw a picture of themselves. In the thought bubble above they should draw a picture of their first memory and then complete the sentence.

When this is completed, explain to the children that you would like them to ask two other people who have known them for a long time to describe their first memory of them. This could be of when they were babies, newly born, or the first time they saw them. The children might ask their parents, grandparents, neighbours, aunts or uncles, either in person or by telephone. They should use the information they gather to complete the other two thought bubbles on the photocopiable sheet.

Again encourage them to bring in earlier photographs of themselves to display alongside

some completed photocopiable sheets on the timeline.

The children's parents could also complete a copy of photocopiable page 122, writing and drawing their own first memory and their parents' (the children's grandparents') first memory of them. These could also be added to the timeline.

LOOK HOW WE'VE CHANGED

Teaching content
Lists can help you organise your thoughts. Charts can give you information.

What you need
Photocopiable page 123 (one per group), photographs (already collected), photocopiable page 124, writing and drawing materials.

What to do
Remind the children of the photograph of you as a baby, the photographs of themselves as babies, the completed photocopiable sheet from Session 6, and the enlarged copy of photocopiable page 120, which showed pictures of articles appropriate to different age-groups. Remind them that these all show different stages of growth and development.

Encourage the children to think about what they could do as a baby. List their ideas on the board. Suggestions will probably include sleep,

especially what they *can* do. In the centre they can draw a picture of themselves.

These sheets, along with a recent photograph of the children, form the final part of the timeline and the project has come full circle.

9

PRESENTING OUR MEMORIES PROJECT

W-60-

Teaching content

All the information we have learned can be summarised, explained and presented in a video.

What you need

The children's completed work, video camera.

What to do

In this session a couple of children from each group will prepare for a video presentation. Two children will operate the video with support from an older child or another adult. Organise the children so that they each have a part to play in the presentation. For example:

Child 1 – reads one of the class diaries about 'At the weekend...' and 'Yesterday'.

Child 2 – explains the wall display and reads some of the examples of 'My first day at school'.

Child 3 – explains the wall display of their parents' or grandparents' first day at school and reads a couple of examples.

Child 4 – explains the wall display of the visitors' memories of school and reads one example.

Child 5 – explains the enlarged copy of photocopiable page 120 and the children's charts of themselves when they were younger.

Child 6 – explains the photographs and display of the children's first memories of themselves and reads two examples.

Child 7 – explains the display 'Look how we've changed' and reads some examples.

Child 8 – explains the display 'Look at us now' and reads his or her own example.

All the children can then come together in front of the display and shout 'Look at us now' for the completion of the video.

The video can be shown later at an assembly or open day for parents, or children can take it home to be viewed by each family in turn.

make noises, cry, wet my nappy, drink, wave my arms and legs about.

Ask the children how they have changed since then? Explain to them that in their groups you want them to list ways in which they have changed, using photocopiable page 123. They should note ways they have changed to look at, in what they can do and in what they like. Appoint one child in each group to list the ideas from the other children in the appropriate boxes. Allow the children to begin this task and give each group either a photograph of you as a baby or photographs of children in the group as babies, if available. They should look at these resources to help them identify changes over time – how has this person changed?

When the children have finished, bring the class together to share their ideas with one another. Prompt with questions:

• What did Jamie look like as a baby?
• What does he look like now?
• What can you do now that you couldn't do as a baby?
• What do you like to do now that you didn't like then?

Emphasise the positive points that they have all grown and developed in different and similar ways, that they can all do much more now than they could when they were younger and that they are all capable people who can do various things.

Give each child a copy of photocopiable page 124 and ask them to complete it as a celebration of what they have achieved, what they are like now, what they like to do now and

MY FIRST DAY AT SCHOOL

I felt	I looked
I liked	I didn't like

My mum felt	My teacher was

MEMORIES OF SCHOOL PAST

Name: _____

When you went to school:

We are doing a project on memories and would like to know what you remember about your own school days.

Please could you give us information on the following things:

Subject	Question	Answer

CAN YOU REMEMBER?

Age	Food	Toys	Clothes	Interests
0–1				
2–3				
4–5				
6–7				

ME IN THE PAST

	0–1 year	2–3 years	4–5 years
Favourite food			
Favourite toy			
Favourite place to go			
Favourite clothes			

FIRST MEMORIES OF ME

My ———— first ————
memory of me was ————

My first memory of me was ————

My ———— first ————
memory of me was ————

Me

Scholastic
NON-FICTION WRITING PROJECTS
Workshop

LOOK HOW WE'VE CHANGED

to look at

in what we like

in what we can do

LOOK AT ME NOW

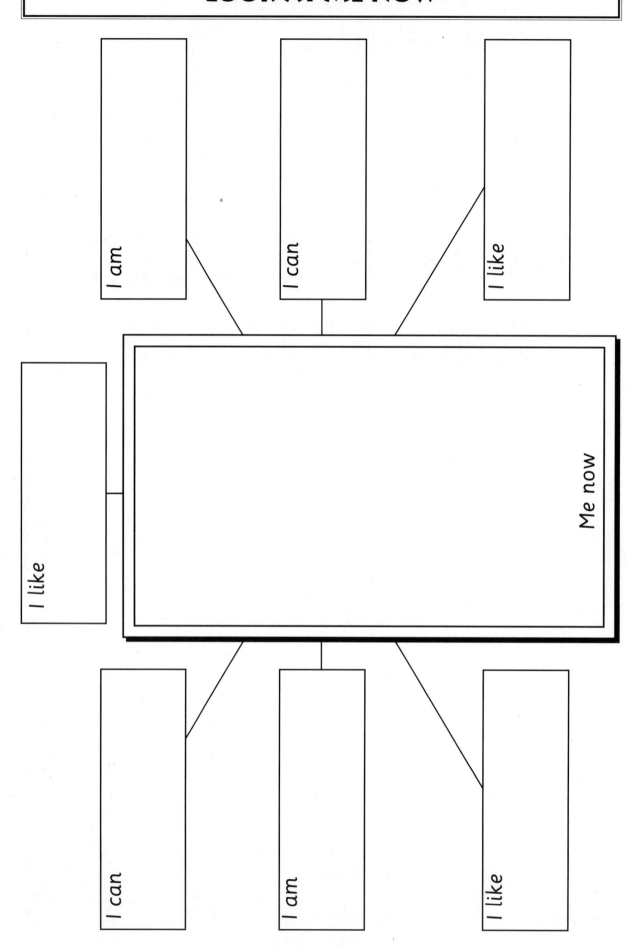

I am

I can

I like

I like

Me now

I can

I am

I like

Chapter Nine

FAIRY TALES
REVISITED

INTRODUCTION

Project description

The starting point for this project is a combination of children's experiences of traditional fairy tales and imaginative play. It begins with the creation of a frieze of Storyland to which the children bring their knowledge of the tales, and information about the characters and different types of houses they would expect to find there. The frieze and its associated labelling provide the backdrop in establishing a Storyland estate agent's office, which provides a context for both emergent writing in free play situations and the variety of genres of writing included within the structured sessions – creating 'All About' books of houses, constructing and replying to letters, designing 'For Sale' posters to persuade people to buy houses in Storyland and justifying reasons in response to a persuasive letter. The project incorporates a storyline of Mr B.B. Wolf wanting to buy a house in Storyland and culminates in an open-ended way with the children deciding on Mr B.B. Wolf's fate!

Why this context?

Children of this age are familiar with most traditional tales. Often a Three Bears' Cottage is set up in the classroom and children participate eagerly in role, using insight into the characters and awareness of the story. This project offers a focus for imaginative play, both free and structured, through the creation of a Storyland estate agent's. The central character of Mr B.B. Wolf is well known to this age group through a variety of different stories. The project aims to enhance children's functional writing through letter-writing activities. It also aims to give them experience in persuading and explaining through an imaginative play context.

Project organisation

Since the focus for this project is an estate agent's office, identify a suitable area for this to be developed with sufficient space for play and a background wall on which to display the Storyland frieze. Children have opportunities to use props, to take on the role of characters and to work in a variety of groupings through play and structured writing activities – individually, in pairs, in small groups and in whole-class situations. At certain points in the project, arrangements are made to 'deliver' letters to the class. The project should take two weeks to complete but children may choose to continue playing in the area for a longer period.

Publication, celebration and review

All writing which is developed through the project is either on display in the estate agent's office or 'sent' to imaginary people. Letters could, however, be displayed or collated in a book. The project ends either with the children welcoming Mr Wolf to their community and encouraging him to buy a house in Storyland, or with Mr Wolf putting forward his case after the residents have voted that he should not be allowed to buy a house there. The open-ended nature of the conclusion gives ownership to the children and they are asked to review their favourite part of the project and to identify the aspects of writing which they liked.

Books the children may find useful

Little Red Riding Hood, Tony Ross (1995) Puffin
Look out He's Behind You, Tony Bradman and Margaret Chamberlain (1988) Mammoth
Princess Smartypants, Babette Cole (1996) Picture Puffin
Prince Cinders, Babette Cole (1989) Picture Lions
Goldilocks and the Three Bears, Michael Rosen (1989) Firefly Books
The Three Billy Goats Gruff, Jonathan Langley (1993) Picture Lions
The Jolly Postman, Janet and Allan Ahlberg (1995) Heinemann
Mr Wolf's Week, Colin Hawkins (1995) Mammoth

Scholastic
NON-FICTION WRITING PROJECTS
Workshop

PRE-SESSION

The children should be familiar with many traditional fairy tales, such as the stories of Goldilocks and the Three Bears, Little Red Riding Hood and Sleeping Beauty. In the days leading up to the project it would be useful to read or tell some of these stories, or to let the children recount them. Discuss the different versions of the stories – do they always end the same way? Are the pictures always similar? In what ways do the versions differ?

Ask the children to think of one character who might live in Storyland (the land of traditional fairy tales) and to draw a picture of his or her house. They should do this at home using photocopiable page 134. Parents should be encouraged to help, if possible, by talking about the pictures with their children.

1

WHO HAS A HOUSE IN STORYLAND?

W → 60

Teaching content

Providing information about individual houses to label a frieze.

What you need

Children's completed copies of photocopiable page 134, photocopiable page 135, a large sheet of paper, marker pens, scissors, adhesive, writing materials.

What to do

Begin by asking the children to bring the pictures they have drawn to the gathering area. Look at each picture in turn and make a tally chart of how many children drew a picture of each character's house.

CHARACTER	HOW MANY?
Three bears	IIII
Cinderella	~~IIII~~ III

Select one fairy tale character and tell the children who drew this character's house to come to the front of the classroom and to hold up their pictures so that others can see them. Then ask the children:

- What type of house is it? (For example, a cottage/palace/castle/small house.)
- How many rooms do you think it has? (One/some/lots.)
- Is there anything special about it? (Tall towers/made of straw/big chimney/covered in sweets.)
- Where do you think it might be in Storyland? (In the woods/near the water/beside a hill.)

As the children give their answers, scribe their ideas on a large sheet of paper under the headings:

- Type
- Rooms
- Anything special?
- Where is it?

There can be various answers for each category. For example, if one child thinks Cinderella's home is a castle and another thinks it is a palace both answers can be written down.

Choose other drawings to discuss, and continue the process until all the children have had an opportunity to contribute their ideas and you have created an adequate list. Explain that you are gathering information about their drawings in order for them to make a big frieze of Storyland.

When you have completed this part of the session, give each child a copy of photocopiable page 135 and tell them that their first task is to write down the name of the character, whose house they have drawn, in the box at the top of the sheet. Then explain that they should circle the type of house, how many rooms and where it is, and write down anything special about it. Model this using one child's drawing as an example.

When the children have finished, tell them to cut out the pictures they drew at home and stick them on to the space provided on the sheet. Retain the sheets for use in the next session.

2

OUR OWN FRIEZE OF STORYLAND

Teaching content
A label can provide information to tell others something about each house in Storyland.

What you need
A classroom helper if possible, writing, drawing and painting materials, sponges for background painting, photocopiable page 136 enlarged to A3, sheets of paper suitable for a frieze, different sizes of paper, card for labels, adhesive, children's completed photocopiable page 135.

What to do
Bring the class together and review the information that was generated in the previous session. The relevant facts are:
- the characters who exist in Storyland;
- the types of houses that they live in;
- the number of rooms;
- locations;
- any special features.

Show the children the enlarged copy of photocopiable page 136 and ask them to identify the various characters' houses. 'Are there any on the sheet that they didn't draw?' Talk about who lives where, the different types of houses and how they compare with the children's drawings. Explain that the children are going to work together to create a big picture frieze of Storyland, using all the information they have gathered.

Group the class according to the characters' houses that they drew initially. Aim for groups of three working together to paint each house for the Storyland frieze. (If too many groups are drawing the same character's house, suggest that the children draw different pictures so that

a variety of houses are represented on the frieze.) Hand out paper and painting materials and allow the children to use their initial drawings to help them with their paintings.

Select a group of four or five children to work on sponge-printing the background grass and sky for the frieze. Choose other children to paint some trees for the woods. Allocate tasks to ensure that all the children are able to contribute. This will be a busy session which you may prefer to undertake on a group basis over a period of a few days rather than organising the whole class. A helper in the class would be

a great advantage. Time will be needed for all painting to be dried and collated on the frieze.

When the children have completed their pictures ask each group to discuss them and write a label that can be placed beside their house painting. This should contain one piece of information such as 'Sleeping Beauty's castle has high walls' or 'Cinderella's palace has lots of windows'. You may wish to write the beginning of the label and allow the children to complete it on their own.

When all the children are ready, bring them together and tell them that when their paintings are dry, they can stick their pictures and labels on to the frieze. Finally, remind the children of the photocopiable sheets they completed in the previous session. Staple together all those pages belonging to the Three Bears, Little Red Riding Hood, and so on to create a book.

Let the children write the title, sign their names as authors and work together to design

All About
The Three Bears' Cottage
by

a border. These can be displayed on a table beside the frieze.

Before the next session, display the background frieze of Storyland in a location in the classroom which can be used in a play situation as an estate agent's office.

3
A LETTER ARRIVES!
W 45

Teaching content
Generating an appropriate list of what may be found in an estate agent's office. Setting up a play area.

What you need
Photocopiable page 137, envelope correctly addressed to the classroom and school, large sheet of paper, marker pens, estate agents' 'For Sale' notices, messenger, props and items to set up an estate agent's office.

What to do
Prior to this session, arrange for someone to deliver the letter on photocopiable page 137 to the classroom in a sealed envelope at the start of the session, saying that it has just arrived for your class.

Begin by praising the children for the work they have done on the Storyland frieze. When the letter arrives, show the children the envelope and ask who they think it may be from. Open

it and read the contents aloud to the class.

Pose the problem – 'What will we do now? How can we help the Wolf?' The children may suggest:
• writing back and saying 'No' to Mr B.B. Wolf;
• asking what kind of house he wants;
• writing to Mr Wolf telling him about the houses on the frieze.

Discuss with the children where people go if they want to buy a house. Hopefully children may suggest a special shop or may even know that it is called an estate agent's. This will largely depend on their previous experience. Explain that this is where people can buy a house and that advertisements for houses are often placed in newspapers or displayed in the windows of estate agents' offices. If you have managed to obtain some 'For Sale' notices show them to the children at this point.

Ask the children what else might be found in an estate agent's office and list their suggestions on a large sheet of paper. These may include:
• leaflets telling you about houses for sale;
• forms to fill in;
• pictures of houses;
• maps or plans of where the houses are;
• telephones, note pads to take messages, cards with people's names, and so on.

Suggest that if an estate agent's office is set up in the classroom, the children could play at being Mr Big Bad Wolf or other fairy tale characters who come in trying to buy a house.

For the next session, ask the children to think about what they might write in a letter to Mr Wolf to inform him of their estate agent's office

and to request further information about the type of property he is looking for.

Setting up the estate agent's

There is much to be gained by involving children in setting up a play area. The stimulus should already have been provided by introducing the context, the background frieze of Storyland and the problem of Mr B.B. Wolf.

Before the next session, use the information and ideas generated by the children to set up an estate agent's area. Provide any necessary props such as a red cape, a Mr B.B. Wolf mask, bears' ears or headbands, and so on, to allow the children to play-act various characters.

This provides an ideal opportunity to involve the children in making or adding to a list of 'People we can be in Storyland'. Items such as a telephone, a note pad and an album of pictures of Storyland houses could all be included to enhance the children's experiences of functional writing through a play situation.

You may wish to organise structured tasks and role-play situations by using character cards on which are written various characters or scenarios, for example 'I am an estate agent' or 'I would like to look at some of your houses for sale'. You may also consider balancing the children's play experiences with free-play situations, giving limited structure, to allow them time to become familiar with the estate agent's area that they have created.

Teaching content

Composing a letter – a letter will identify who is being addressed, give information and be signed at the end by the sender.

What you need

Photocopiable page 137 from the previous session, photocopiable page 138, A4 paper, scissors, adhesive, large sheet of paper, marker pens, writing and drawing materials.

What to do

Read Mr B.B. Wolf's letter again to the children. Stress the main point – that he wants to buy a house in Storyland. Ask the children what they think they should write in a letter of reply to Mr Wolf, especially as the estate agent's office has now been set up in the classroom.

Model the activity for the children by demonstrating the component parts of a letter. Explain that in the top right-hand corner of a letter is written the sender's address. Write this on a large sheet of paper using the school address or that of the estate agent's office. Show Mr B.B. Wolf's letter again and explain that he probably did not write his address because he has not got a house yet!

Point to the introduction in Mr Wolf's letter and make comparisons:

- Dear Class ___ – ask the children how they will reply.
- Mr Wolf gave information about wanting a house – what information will the children give?
- The letter was signed by Mr B.B. Wolf – how will the children sign their response to him?

Show the children photocopiable page 138 and explain that on it are written some suggestions for starting the letter, giving information and saying who it is from. Organise the children into pairs, hand out a copy of the photocopiable sheet, scissors, adhesive and one sheet of A4 paper. Tell the children to choose what they want to say, cut out the relevant sections, stick them on their sheet of A4 paper and add any other information that they feel should be passed on to Mr Wolf. You may need to scribe for some children. When they have finished, the children can draw a picture on their sheet to accompany their message

Photocopy the children's letters when they have been completed. Bring the class back together and read some of these aloud or let the children read them to each other. Put all of the letters in a large envelope addressed to Mr B.B. Wolf! Remind the children that Mr Wolf had not given his address. Ask the children to brainstorm some possible locations, for example 'The Forest', 'Big Bad Street', 'Wolf Road'.

HOUSES FOR SALE

Teaching content
Selecting key points of information to advertise the sale of a house and persuade others to buy. Identifying relevant reasons for buying a house.

What you need
A selection of 'For Sale' notices from property magazines/estate agents' lists, photocopiable page 139, large sheet of paper, marker pens, thin black felt-tipped pens, writing and drawing materials.

What to do
Note: This session may be most effectively implemented working with one group at a time, perhaps over a few days, to ensure that all children have an opportunity to make a 'For

Sale' poster with your input.

At the end of the previous session, the children had replied to Mr B.B. Wolf's letter. Explain that since he is looking for a house, other characters in Storyland may be looking also. Tell the children that in this session they are going to try to persuade people to buy a house in Storyland and are going to make 'For Sale' posters to put up in their estate agent's office. Remind children of the 'For Sale' notices that they looked at in Session 3.

Show the children the 'For Sale' notices you have obtained. Although they will be unable to read all of the details, try to elicit some of the key features of the layout. For instance:
- the name of the estate agent;
- a picture of the property;
- the address of the house;
- the price;
- information about both the outside and the inside of the house.

Explain to the children that you would like them to think about a new house that could go in Storyland. It may be like some others that are already there or it could be completely different. Organise the children into pairs and ask them to discuss:
- what the house would look like outside and inside;
- who might want to buy it;
- what would make people want to buy it.

After the children have had some talking time, model the activity yourself by drawing a picture of a potential house for sale. For instance, you could draw a picture of a palace with lots of windows in it and tell the children that this would be a good house for Cinderella's sisters

because they want to be like her and live in a palace with lots of windows so they can be seen. Then tell the children that you are going to write down three good things about the house. For example, it has:

• mirrors for the sisters to admire themselves;
• large rooms to hold a grand ball;
• large fitted wardrobes for all the clothes they wear.

Write these points on a large sheet of paper. When you feel the children have understood,

move on to looking at other examples of ideal properties for fairy tale characters. For example:
• Mr B.B. Wolf – a house without a chimney or fireplace;
• Grandma's cottage – a big locked gate so that wolves can't get in;
• Billy Goats Gruff – a piece of land with lots of green grass to eat, far away from bridges;
• house of bricks – can't be blown down, big enough for three occupants;
• large cottage – good for Snow White and lots of dwarves – has eight bedrooms.

Tell the children to choose a property for a character.

Give each child a copy of photocopiable page 139 and tell them to draw their picture in the box using a thin black felt-tipped pen, adding as much detail as possible. They may choose to colour it in later. When they have drawn their picture ask them to complete the writing. They should write who their house is for and why, and then list three features of the

house that would make it particularly appealing to that character.

Paste some of the completed posters beside the frieze in the estate agent's office and keep others in a filing box, to add to the play when 'characters' come in to ask for a house.

NO WOLVES HERE!

Teaching content

Stating a case and giving reasons to persuade others. Writing a letter to justify a point of view.

What you need

Photocopiable pages 140 and 141, large sheet of paper divided vertically with the heading 'Mr Wolf should have a house because...' written on one side and 'Mr Wolf should not have a house because...' written on the other side, writing and drawing materials.

What to do

As with Session 3, arrange for a messenger to deliver the letter on photocopiable page 140 to the classroom. Gather the children together and read it aloud. Pose the problem – 'What do we do now?' Ask the children to tell the person sitting next to them whether they think that Mr B.B. Wolf should be allowed to buy a house. Or do they think he should not, on any condition, be allowed to buy a house? Ask them to give their reasons.

Record the children's points of view and their reasons on your large sheet of paper under the appropriate headings. The children will probably suggest various reasons. Make sure they are all given equal consideration. Conclude the session by voting on how many children think Mr Wolf should have a house.

For the final part of this session, the children should reply individually to the residents of Storyland using photocopiable page 141 to give the decision that was made. You may have to explain how to complete the message by circling or deleting the words 'should/should not'. Children can then copy one of the reasons you have listed on your large sheet or write one of their own and draw a picture.

The concluding session will depend on the outcome of the vote!

7

WELCOME MR WOLF OR MR WOLF HAS HIS SAY

Teaching content

Role-play based on the decisions made and points of view expressed in the previous session. Celebration and review – evaluating the project.

What you need

A5 card to make a badge, ribbon, an adult to take the role of Mr B.B. Wolf, writing and drawing materials, photocopiable page 142, lemonade or other soft drink, paper cups.

What to do

This final session should be played in role to bring the project to a conclusion.

Ensure that all the children are fully involved in this project by making a badge which they can wear during the session. This can be made using A5 sized card with holes punched in it, through which a piece of ribbon can be threaded. The children can then wear these round their necks.

Tell the children that for the final part of the project they can choose to be any character in Storyland – except Mr B.B. Wolf. Hand out the badges and explain that they are to draw a picture of themselves as a character from a fairy tale and write the character's name and where they live in Storyland. For instance, 'I am Jack and I live at the foot of the Beanstalk.'

With the estate agent's office set up and children having had the opportunity to play between the structured sessions, the arrival of Mr B.B. Wolf should lead to a logical conclusion.

In assuming the role of Mr Wolf ensure that the props with which the children are familiar are used, such as the bears' ears, a red cape, and so on. Tell the children that they are going to be the residents of Storyland and you are going to be Mr B.B. Wolf.

Arrange for a group to take on the roles of staff within the estate agent's. The rest of the children should be the residents of Storyland. If the conclusion to the previous session was that Mr Wolf should be allowed to buy a house in Storyland, Mr Wolf can:
• thank the residents and the people in the estate agent's;
• talk with the children about the best house to buy and what he is looking for in a suitable house;
• promise to be an upstanding member of the community;
• celebrate his new house with 'Wolf' lemonade!

If, however, the residents or Storyland decided that Mr Wolf should not be allowed to buy a house, role-play Mr Wolf putting forward his point of view. This scenario may end with Mr Wolf leaving and the 'residents' celebrating with lemonade as he goes!

When everyone has come out of role, ask the children which part of the project they enjoyed most and why. Give each child a copy of photocopiable page 142 and ask them to complete it. When they have done so, the pages can be collated into a class book.

Finally, ask the children to choose an appropriate title for the book and write this on the front cover. The estate agent's office should remain in the class for as long as the children are motivated by the storyline of this project.

IN STORYLAND

Dear Parent,

In the next few weeks Class ___ will be involved in a lot of activities about Storyland, the land of traditional fairy tales, and the characters who live there, such as Goldilocks, Little Red Riding Hood and Snow White.

   Please encourage your child to draw a picture of the house of one of these characters and talk about the type of house it is. Maybe it is a castle with big walls and lots of windows, or a cottage with small rooms.

   We will use these pictures to make a big classroom frieze of Storyland.

Thank you

WHAT IS IT LIKE?

All about [_____] house

What type of house?	cottage	palace	other
How many rooms?	one	a few	lots
Where is it?	in the woods	near the river	other

Is there anything special about it?

FAIRY TALE HOMES

Scholastic
NON-FICTION WRITING PROJECTS
Workshop

A LETTER ARRIVES!

Dear Class————

I hear that you have been making a picture of Storyland.

I would really like to move into the area and wonder if you could find me a house there.

I have found this difficult in the past. There has been a lot of huffing and puffing about it by the residents of Storyland.

I can assure you that I would be a good and caring neighbour. All I ask for is a little house somewhere quiet in Storyland.

Could you please help me?

From
Mr B.B. Wolf

LET'S WRITE BACK

_____ School

Dear Big Bad Wolf

We have read your letter.

We have an estate agent's office in our class.

We need to know the type of house you want.

We would like to know where you would like to live in Storyland.

from

Class _____ Estate Agent
Buyahouse Street
Storyland

Dear Mr B.B. Wolf

Thank you for your letter.

We have made a picture of Storyland in our class.

Please come to visit our estate agent's office.

We are sure that we will find you a house.

from

Class _____ Estate Agents

Scholastic
NON-FICTION WRITING PROJECTS
Workshop

HOUSES FOR SALE

Storyland Estate Agent
FOR SALE

This is a good house for _____

because _____

It has:

*

*

*

NO WOLVES HERE!

Storyland Residents' Association
Fairy tale Avenue
Storyland

Dear Class _____ ,

We have heard that you are acting on behalf of Mr B.B. Wolf who is looking for a house in this area.

We in Storyland do not think that he should move here. In the past he has been known to blow down houses, dress up in other people's clothes, hide behind trees and frighten our neighbours.

Please take our request seriously and do NOT sell one of your houses to Mr B.B. Wolf.

From
The residents of Storyland

Scholastic
NON-FICTION WRITING PROJECTS
Workshop

HERE'S OUR REPLY

Storyland Estate Agents
Buyahouse Street
Storyland

Dear residents of Storyland,

We have decided that Mr B.B.Wolf should/should not buy a house in Storyland because

Thank you for your interest.
From

WHAT I ENJOYED

My favourite part of this project was

because

I liked writing

Chapter Ten

TIME ALL AROUND

INTRODUCTION

Project description

This project begins by inviting children to look for evidence of aspects of time in the environment – on the way home from school and in their houses. They are asked to look for four items which give information about time and its function. Feedback from this activity is then collated to create a display which draws on the children's experiences. The creation of the display is the focal point for this project. Children are then encouraged to bring in pictures, photographs, clocks or watches, if allowed, in order to talk about these and devise questions to ask of others to gain more information. The next series of activities offer everyday situations that will help children to realise that time is not just about clocks, but is an intrinsic part of life and can be recorded in different functional writing formats. The project ends with the children assessing the display to which they have all contributed.

Why this context?

Time is a concept which children develop awareness of gradually, and in order to understand it they need to be encouraged to relate the passage of time to their own experiences. 'Time All Around' provides an ideal context as work on time is part of the daily routine of a classroom. This project enables children to link their own experiences of time with functional writing and mathematics. Through a series of activities, children will be involved in developing their skills by making lists, devising questions and answers, creating information labels, recounting present and past events, reporting, sequencing information, logging events in a diary and producing TV timetables.

Project organisation

As the central focus for the project will be a display, an area will be required for this purpose. It would be useful to provide one or two tables upon which items brought in by you and the children may be displayed. A wall or display board will also be necessary. Some additional materials, such as photographs or pictures of time in the environment, will enhance the stimulus for this project. For example, shop opening times, postboxes, train departure timetables and certainly a few clocks or watches which represent time in different ways would encourage talking and writing. The project is organised to enable a variety of grouping arrangements – whole class, groups, pairs and individuals. The emphasis will be on all children contributing to the display.

The project may be free-standing or may be part of a class topic in mathematics.

Publication, celebration and review

In the final session, children will have an opportunity to review all of the writing and variety of formats used to produce the display – question and answer labels, 'Times in Our Lives' in a book, 'Times at School' strung across the room, diaries stored in a box and group posters of what can be achieved in a minute. The display should be photographed to enable each child to have a memento of the project. With their own written evaluation of the project, this can be taken home to share with their family.

Books the children may find useful

I Wonder Why the Sun Rises: And Other Questions About Time and Seasons, Brenda Walpole (1996) Kingfisher

Knowabout Time, Henry Pluckrose (1987) Franklin Watts

What's the Time?, Richard and Nicky Hales (1991) Cherrytree

Take Off With Time, Sally Hewitt (1995) Evans Brothers Ltd

PRE-SESSION

Organise an area within the classroom to be the focal point for displaying the children's work arising from this project. If you wish to keep it very simple the area need only contain a display board and tables.

Introduce the project by showing the children the area and explaining that in the next few weeks they are going to be involved in creating a display about 'Time All Around'.

Hand out photocopiable page 152 and read through the sheet with the children. Explain that they need to look out for four objects or items which indicate time. This can be things they see on the way home or in their houses. Tell them that in the left-hand column on the sheet they should draw a picture of what they see and in the right-hand column they should write what it does. For example, a microwave clock times how long it takes to cook something and a postbox tells you when letters will be collected. The top of the sheet explains the project to the child's family.

Ask the children to complete this for the first session and bring it to school.

WHERE DO WE SEE TIME?

ⓦ→♦♦♦♦ 🕛

Teaching content
Creating a list of items which give information about time and its purpose.

What you need
Children's completed copies of photocopiable page 152, large sheets of paper, marker pens, scissors, adhesive.

What to do
Gather the class together to collate their responses to the pre-session task. On a large sheet of paper, begin by listing items the children saw which indicated the time in some way. This will probably generate a list of common items such as clocks, watches, cookers, microwaves, video-recorders, and so on. Next, ask the children if they can add to this list by thinking of other places where they might see items which give information about time, for instance train and airport arrival and departure boards, a town hall clock, timetables. Add their suggestions to the list.

Ask the children what all of these items do and how they help to give us information about time. Write these on the right-hand side of the list. Suggestions may include:

An alarm clock	wakes you up in the morning.
A microwave	rings a bell when food is cooked.
A railway timetable	tells you when trains arrive and depart.
A television schedule	tells you when programmes start and finish.
A stopwatch	times how long it takes to run from one place to another.

Organise the children into four groups and give each group one large sheet of paper and some scissors. Ask them to cut out the items from their photocopiable sheets and arrange these down the left-hand side of the large sheet, grouping together those that are the same or similar. On the right-hand side, tell the children to arrange the sections in which they wrote about how these items give information about time. When you have checked that everything is in the correct position, allow the children to stick their pieces of paper on to the sheet. Hand out two or three blank squares for them to write down any further examples of time that they may think of.

The groups' sheets, plus the collated list from the beginning of the activity, should be displayed to form the background for further work. For the next session, ask the children to bring in any pictures, advertisements or photographs of items which show the time. If the children have personal watches or clocks at home ask them to seek permission from their parents to bring them into school. Reassure them that you will be bringing items to school for those who may not find anything at home.

2

TELL ME ABOUT...

Teaching content

Devising questions to ask about the objects/pictures brought in and writing factual answers which give information in response.

What you need

Pictures and items which depict the time, a special object of your own, photocopiable page 153, sheets of A4 card folded in half horizontally, scissors, adhesive, writing materials.

What to do

Ask the children to place the objects or pictures which they have brought in on their tables. Show your special object to the children, briefly describing it. For example, if your object is a watch, explain where you got it, any special features it has or that you particularly like, whether it is digital or analogue, and so on. Ask the children if they have any questions about its appearance, what it does or how it helps to tell the time. The emphasis in this session is on enabling children to devise appropriate questions. Draw their attention to the beginnings of questions – 'What', 'Where', 'Why', 'How', and so on.

Repeat the process by asking one child to describe briefly the object he or she has brought in. Some questions may be complicated and lead to answers of 'I don't know': for example, 'What makes the alarm bell ring at 7.30 in the morning?' Depending on the age of the class, you may find it useful to generate a list of 'Things to find out about time' or 'Questions about time' and, using non-fiction books, use this as an appropriate link between information reading and writing. The children's questions could be displayed in the area and form an on-going part of the project

For the final part of the session, organise the class into pairs, ensuring that all the children have an object or picture to talk about. Give each child a copy of photocopiable page 153 to structure this part of the session and explain that each child will take turns to ask questions of the other. One child will first describe her object to her partner. Using the photocopiable sheet, the second child will then write down three questions about the object which he would like answered. The first child then

answers these questions in the spaces provided on the sheet. Together the children review the questions and answers and decide on the most interesting one. This is then written as a final version on the label at the foot of the sheet. The children should complete the heading 'Tell me about...', for instance 'Tell me about Leon's watch'. The question should then be cut out and stuck on to one side of the folded A5 card with the answer pasted on the other side. This information card can be displayed beside the child's object or picture. The process is then repeated with the other child in the pair.

TIMES IN OUR LIVES
ⓦ→♦ 🕐60

Teaching content
Giving information by recounting past and present events and explaining reasons for choosing them.

What you need
Photocopiable page 154, large sheet of paper with the same headings as those on photocopiable page 154, writing materials.

What to do
The emphasis in this session is on time as it affects the individual child. Begin by bringing the class together and explain that they are going to talk about times in their own lives. First of all, ask the children to tell the person sitting next to them what their favourite time is at present and why. This may be a time when they are involved in a hobby they enjoy, when they are watching a television programme they particularly like, when they are playing a game, or it may be more general such as a birthday celebration or Christmas. When the children have had enough time to talk, choose some of their suggestions and record them on the large sheet of paper under the appropriate heading – you may wish to include some of your own favourite times. Repeat this process for a 'favourite time in the past'. This may be either an event or a recurrent time.

When you have done this, give each child a copy of photocopiable page 154 and tell them to complete the first two sections. When they have completed these sections, read out the

next starter sentence, 'I am always early for...'. Again discuss this with the class, recording relevant information on your large sheet of paper, writing both the occasions and the reasons. Tell the children to fill in this section on their photocopiable sheets and then to complete the last three sentences:
- It seems like a long time until...
- I need a long time to...
- I am never late for...

When all the sheets are completed, collate them in a folder entitled 'Times in Our Lives' to add to the display.

TIMES AT SCHOOL
ⓦ→♦♦♦♦ 🕐60

Teaching content
Sequencing information about what happens on each school day using different formats.

What you need
Large sheet of paper (with grid marked Monday, Tuesday, Wednesday, Thursday, Friday, and divided into four sections for each day), three sequence cards (marked 'Before play', 'After play', 'After lunch'), 20 small sheets of card to fit into the grid, string and clothes pegs, marker pens, five sheets of A3 card each labelled with

Monday	Assembly	PE		
Tueasday				
Wednesday				
Thursday				
Friday				

a different school day, Blu-Tack, various sizes/ shapes of paper, writing and drawing materials, class timetables.

What to do

Note: There may already be a timetable or sign within the classroom which identifies what happens at different points of each school day, for example PE, Structured Play, Reading Time, Music, Assembly. This may be a useful starting point to the session.

Gather the class together and show them the blank grid you have prepared and any timetables which may be relevant, for example class timetables. Explain to the class that they are going to create an information sheet which will tell others about four things that they do on each day of the school week. Choose an example, such as PE, and ask the children when they go to it. Write 'PE' on one of the small pre-cut cards and attach it beside the appropriate day on the grid. (Alternatively, you may prefer to draw a symbol to signify PE.) Repeat with other lessons and activities until all 20 spaces have been filled. Next introduce the sequence cards and explain that it is important that information is given in the order in which the events occur. In this case, what happens

first (before play), next (after play) and last (after lunch). Reorganise the cards for each day, if necessary, so that the information is displayed sequentially.

Organise the children into five groups, one for each day of the school week. Explain that each group, using A3 card, will organise the information for their particular day in a different way.

Group 1
Children will draw and label the four different events and stick them in order from top to bottom on a sheet of A3 card. See Figure 1.

Group 2
The four events should be drawn and labelled and stuck to the A3 sheet, with arrows indicating the correct sequence, to form a flow diagram. Figure 2 gives an example of how it could look.

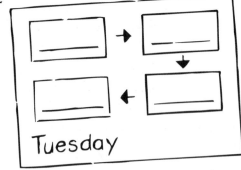

Figure 1

Figure 2

Group 3
Each event should be drawn in one quarter of a circle and glued on to the sheet with the first event at the top. A label should be pasted next to each activity. See Figure 3.

Figure 3

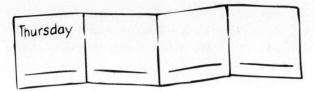

Figure 4

Group 4

Each event is drawn and labelled on to one page of a zigzag book as in Figure 4.

Group 5

The four events are drawn, labelled and pasted on to the sheet in a horizontal line. See Figure 5.

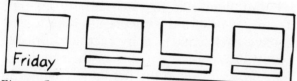

Figure 5

When each group has completed their sheet, peg these to a piece of string or a washing line across the room near to the 'Time All Around' display.

5

TIMES AT HOME – MY WEEKEND DIARY

Teaching content

Recounting events in sequence. Using a diary format.

What you need

One booklet for each child, consisting of five sheets of A5 paper stapled at the side, a diary, writing and drawing materials.

What to do

Note: If possible, try to carry out this session on a Friday.

Remind the children of the work they did in the previous session, in which they drew up various timetables for school activities. Explain that in this session they will be planning a diary consisting of four events that occurred over a weekend period. Ask the children if they know what a diary is and what goes in it. 'Why do some people write in a diary? What might they write? Who usually reads a diary?'

Explain that the purpose of the diaries they will be keeping is to tell their classmates about four interesting events that occurred over the weekend. Ask the children to suggest what these might be. Explain that the diaries will be varied since everyone's weekend will be different, with different events to recount.

Show the children the diary you have brought in and look at the outline of a page. Point out the spaces for the day and date and for writing. Explain that different diaries fulfil different purposes. Establish that some people write things in diaries to remind them to do particular things on a certain day, whereas other people use diaries as a way of remembering different events that have occurred. For example, 'I went to the swimming pool and swam two lengths' or 'I got new trainers. They are white with blue stripes. I bought them with my granny in the big shop on the High Street.'

When you have established with the children what a diary is, and the type of events that can be written about, discuss the concept of sequence. Remind the children that they began to put events into a sequence in the previous session, using the sequence cards 'Before play', 'After play' and 'After lunch'. Ask the children if it would be sensible to begin with something that happened on Sunday night and follow it with an event that occurred on Saturday morning. Emphasise that the four events they choose will need to be written in chronological order. Stress that you do not want the children to write down the events, as they will be doing this in school, but to think of the four events that they would like to use.

When the children return to school it would be useful to start the task early in the morning while the events the children have chosen are still fresh in their memories. Give the children the booklets you have prepared and tell them to open them and write about one event on each page. (The children should start on the second page as they will be drawing an illustration on the front cover.) Explain that they should write the day and the date when the event occurred at the top of each sheet. Remind them that they must write about their events in the correct sequential order. They can also draw a picture to illustrate each one. When the children have completed their book, explain that they should design a front cover and give their diary a title.

All of the children's diaries may then be stored in a box labelled 'Our Weekend Diaries' and displayed on the 'Time' table.

TELEVISION TIMES

Teaching content
Giving information in a timetable format. Justifying selection of programmes and their order.

What you need
A selection of TV listings magazines, photocopiable page 155, large sheet of paper (marked 4.00pm, 4.30pm, 5.00pm, 5.30pm and so on to 8.00pm), strips of paper, writing and drawing materials, Blu-Tack.

What to do
Gather the class together and ask them which TV programmes, if any, they watched when they arrived home from school on the previous day. List some of their answers on strips of paper and attach them to the board or a large sheet of paper. Next show the children the sheet marked in half-hourly intervals which you have prepared. Select individual children to take the strips of paper on which you have written the television programmes and rearrange them in the order in which they appeared on the television. Anything after 8.00pm could be recorded at the foot of the page.

Open one of the TV listings magazines at a page showing a daily schedule. Ask the children what kind of information this gives. They may suggest:

- the name of the programme;
- when it is on;
- who is in it;
- how long it lasts;
- whether it is a 'repeat';
- which channel it is on.

Explain to the children that they are going to create their own list of favourite programmes, but they can choose only four. They must decide which programme they would like to watch between 4.00pm and 5.30pm and write why they would like to watch it. Hand out some TV magazines for the children to refer to.

Give each child a copy of photocopiable page 155 and ask them to write their choice of four programmes in the left-hand column. In the right-hand column they should write their reasons for choosing these programmes. When they have finished their writing they can decorate the border with drawings of characters from their favourite TV programmes. Try to make time for the children to read their sheets to each other before displaying them in the 'Time All Around' area. If there is insufficient wall space, the children's work can be collated in a ring-binder folder. A small group could be selected to design a front cover of favourite TV times for this.

TIME YOURSELF!

Teaching content
Reporting what children can do in one minute.

What you need
Three one-minute timers or stop clocks, oval shaped paper, large sheet labelled 'In one minute...', marker pens, writing materials.

What to do
The concept of the passing of time, and in particular the concept of a minute, can often be difficult for children. This session aims to enable children to investigate what they can do in a minute and to report their findings to others and record them on a group sheet. (For

When the activity is over, bring the children together and ask what each achieved. Hand out the oval-shaped paper on to which each child should write what they did.

I clapped my hands 42 times

Cheryl

Display these around the large group sheet and add it to the wall display. The activity can be repeated and comparisons made with other groups in the class.

8
THE 'TIME ALL AROUND' DISPLAY
Ⓦ ⏱60

Teaching content
Reviewing the display, evaluating and justifying children's favourite pieces of writing.

What you need
Loaded camera, photocopiable page 156, writing materials.

What to do
Gather the children so that they can all see their collated work on display – the 'time' objects and pictures, question and answer labels, box of 'Times in Our Lives' sheets, 'Times at School' display, diaries, TV timetables and 'In one minute...' sheets. Ask each child in turn to tell the others which was their favourite piece of writing and why.

Tell the children that since so much effort has gone into the display, you are going to take a photograph of it for each of them to keep. Hand out photocopiable page 156 and ask the children to write about which part of the project they enjoyed writing the most and what other aspects of time they would write about if there were more space – and time!

The top box should be reserved for the photograph when developed. The sheet can be backed on to card or mounted and taken home to share with the child's family.

organisational purposes, you may find it easier to carry out this activity with one group at a time rather than the whole class.)

Tell the children to close their eyes and only open them when they think a minute has passed. (If some children open their eyes before a minute has passed, signal to them to close them again until a minute is up.) When a minute has passed, tell the children to open their eyes and ask them how they calculated a minute – this can often be very interesting. Now ask the children what they think they could do in one minute. For example, how many times could they clap their hands or write their name? How far could they walk down the corridor? Brainstorm with the children other ideas for things that could be assessed in one minute and write these on the labelled sheet of paper.

Organise the children into pairs and tell them to choose one of the activities to carry out. Give them some thinking time in which to decide which activity to choose. (Obviously you will have to be responsive to the management of children who may need to undertake an activity outside the classroom and any materials they may need.) It would be helpful for each pair to carry out a different activity.

When they have decided, one child should carry out the activity while the other times a minute using a timer or stop clock. Allow time for both children to have an opportunity to carry out the activity.

TIME ALL AROUND

We will be carrying out a writing project about 'Time All Around' over the next few weeks and would be grateful for any clocks, watches (not valuable!), pictures or photographs you may have to help the children create a display.

On the way home and this evening, your child will be looking for four items which give information about time, such as clocks, times on postboxes, open and closed signs in shops, television times, and so on. Using the space below they should draw and name the item in the left-hand column and briefly write its purpose in the right-hand column. Thank you for your help.

I saw	This is what it does

TELL ME ABOUT...

Question	Answer

Tell me about _____

Question

Answer

TIMES IN OUR LIVES

Times in my life by _____

My favourite time is
because
My favourite time was
because
I am always early for
because
It seems like a long time until
I need a long time to
I am never late for

Scholastic
NON-FICTION WRITING PROJECTS
Workshop

MY FAVOURITE TV TIMES

At	I would watch	because
4.00pm		
4.30pm		
5.00pm		
5.30pm		

TIME ALL AROUND

Stick your photograph here

I liked writing about

If we had more time I would like to write about

Scholastic WORKSHOP

Chapter Eleven

CHANGES

INTRODUCTION

Project description

In this project children work together to compile a group book of changes. At the end of the project these are donated to the school library and other infant classes. The children carry out research into changes in the natural world, both animals and plants, and changes in people. The focus is on children gaining knowledge and information about the different kinds of change and passing this on in an appropriate way to others.

Why this context?

The focus of this project, 'Changes', is a relatively abstract concept which covers many things: day into night, seasonal changes, growth, change in the animal world such as metamorphosis, changes in people – their moods, feelings and behaviour. Writers on children's thinking recognise that children often make connections or make sense of the world in more abstract ways than adults may expect. This context provides the opportunity for children to follow up a line of inquiry on the more abstract focus of change.

Young children are eager to learn facts and find explanations and justifications. This project is focused on content: things for children to learn about and learn from. It offers opportunities for children to use their own experiences and then to look beyond them by researching in books and then recording their learning and transmitting it to others.

Change can seem a threatening thing to everybody, for example the birth of a new baby, a new house or school, a new child in class. Change is, however, natural to life and in investigating change children may come to understand that it is natural and that we can learn to accept it and adjust to it.

The project offers a wide range of opportunities for the development of functional writing. Children recount personal experiences of change, report on information they find out, explain experiments they carry out, research various types of changes for their book and construct front and back covers, contents, indexes and glossaries. This involves children in writing reports, explanations, lists, plans and diagrams, instructions – a suitably, varied list for this project with an older infant class.

Project organisation

For much of this project the whole class is organised into mixed ability groups of about six. These groups remain as working units throughout the project.

The groups come together in the larger class group for explanations of techniques or giving of information and reporting back on research or findings in experiments. Children also work individually to contribute to each page of the group book. Each task is tightly structured towards the end product: the group book for Reception/P1, Year 1/P2 or the library.

Before the start of the project, organise the class into mixed ability groups of 6-8 and explain they are going to make a book.

Publication, celebration and review

Each group publishes an information book to be used by younger children in other classes and for the school library. The children will feel a sense of achievement at working collaboratively on a project, sharing out tasks and decision-making and creating an end-product – a book – which will be used by other people and be helpful to them. The project ends with the children evaluating the effectiveness of all aspects of their information book with other classes.

Books the children may find useful

Changes, Joanne Jessop (1992) Wayland
Tadpole and Frog, Chicken and Egg, Butterfly and Caterpillar, Broad Bean Christine Back and Barrie Watts (1994) A&C Black
The Apple Trees, Caterpillar, Caterpillar, Vivian French (1996) Walker Books
The Very Hungry Caterpillar, The Tiny Seed, Eric Carle (1974) Puffin
Starting History Series, *Our schools*, (1994), *Our family* (1992) and *Where we lived* (1994) Stewart Ross, Wayland

CHANGES – WHAT? HOW? WHY?

W → ↑↑↑↑ 60

Teaching content
Information can be recorded in pictures, using signs/symbols and words.

What you need
Photocopiable page 120 (enlarged to A3), photocopiable page 171, a selection of reference books (see 'Books the children may find useful'), strips of paper 20cm × 5cm, A3 cartridge paper, writing and drawing materials, marker pens, adhesive.

What to do
Gather the class together and focus their attention on your enlarged copy of photocopiable page 120. Ask the children what it tells them. Prompt them with questions to help them interpret the sheet more closely.
• What did the baby like to play with?
• What about the toddler?
• What about the school child?
Elicit from them the fact that what the child likes to play with has changed as he or she has grown older. Ask further questions such as:
• What did the baby like to eat?
• What about the toddler?
• What about the school child?

Again, note the fact that what the child likes to eat has changed. Concentrate on the children themselves by asking if they think they have changed since they were babies and toddlers. Try to focus their ideas on how they looked then and now, what they could do when they were younger and what they can do now, and where they liked to go when they were babies and toddlers compared to where they like to go now. Emphasise that all these things have changed because they have changed. Ask them 'How have you changed? What has happened to you?' The children should recognise that they have grown up, and by growing older and stronger they have changed in lots of ways.

Ask the children to consider whether growth or growing is the only kind of change there is. Prompt them with questions such as 'Does the world around you change? How?' Try to elicit from them that there are night and day, seasons

and types of weather, and establish that many things change quite naturally. Ask the children whether animals change. Hopefully they will recognise that animals, like people, grow. Take any other ideas if they are forthcoming, for example the children may suggest that some animals can change colour or shape such as a tadpole becoming a frog. Ask if plants change. Again, the children will recognise that plants grow, leaves change colour, trees and plants show seasonal changes, and so on.

Organise the children into groups of approximately eight and appoint one child in each group to be the group leader. Give each group a copy of photocopiable page 171 and tell them that you would like them all to complete it.

Model an example for the children. Look at the first category which refers to changes in people. Establish with the class that people grow from babies to children then into grown-ups and finally to old people, so this is what the children should write on their sheets. Ask how else people change. The children may suggest that people's moods change, for example from happy to sad, so this too could be written on their photocopiable sheets. Encourage the children to think of their own ideas. Show them the range of books you have gathered and tell them that they can refer to these if they need fresh ideas.

Remind the children that they must complete all the boxes. Tell them that you would like the group leader to note down their ideas in the appropriate columns. Explain that they need not worry too much about spelling as this is just a brainstorm of ideas.

Give the children 10–15 minutes to complete their photocopiable sheets. Circulate around the groups, checking on their progress and helping when required.

When they have finished, explain that each group will be making a book about 'Changes' which will be presented to the school library. Give each child a strip of paper (20cm × 5cm) and tell them to choose a type of change (they should each choose a different one from the other members of their group). On the strip of paper they should record the change in pictures and words. Figure 1 gives an example of how their strips of paper could look.

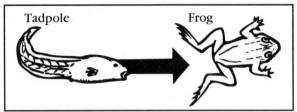

Figure 1

When these are completed to everyone's satisfaction, give each group a sheet of A3 cartridge paper (depending on the number of children in each group they may need two sheets). The group leader, with help from the group, should arrange the pictures on the sheet of A3 and write a heading in pencil such as 'Lots of things change'. At the bottom of the page he or she should write a sentence such as 'Change is natural'. (You can either write these on the board for the chidren to copy or they can create their own sentences.) When everyone is satisfied with the layout, the strips should be stuck on and the written headings gone over in felt-tipped pen or marker. Page 1 of the book is now completed.

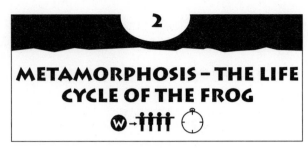

METAMORPHOSIS – THE LIFE CYCLE OF THE FROG

Teaching content
Changes can be shown by a sequence of pictures and labels. You can follow a pictorial sequence of instructions to make something.

What you need
Selection of reference books (see list on page 158, include some that show the process of metamorphosis, particularly from tadpole to frog), A3 cartridge paper, scissors, card (25cm × 25cm), plate (20cm diameter), writing and drawing materials, paper fasteners, photocopiable pages 172, 173 and 174.

What to do
Bring the class together and explain that in this session they will be focusing on one particular change in the animal kingdom. Remind them of the work they did in the previous session and ask whether anyone can remember any major changes which occur in some animals. The children may recall that tadpoles turn into frogs or caterpillars into butterflies. Ask the children if any of them have experience of watching tadpoles change. Do they know the name for this change? Either tell or remind the children that it is called 'metamorphosis'. Ask a child to find a book from the selection you have gathered which depicts the change from tadpole to frog, and read it to the class.

Scholastic
NON-FICTION WRITING PROJECTS
Workshop

When you have finished, work through the various stages in the development of the tadpole. These being:

- frog-spawn;
- tadpole with tail;
- tadpole with legs and tail;
- tadpole with legs and no tail;
- frog.

Organise the children into the same groups as before and give each group leader a copy of photocopiable page 172. Explain that you want five members of each group to record in pictures each stage in the life of a frog. They can use the reference books to help them. Explain that the sequence on the sheet is wrong so the group leader must first cut up the sheet and issue one strip to each child. They should then complete their drawings.

The other members of the groups will work with you to make a 'peep through wheel'. This is explained on photocopiable page 173. (You may like to make a mock-up prior to the session for demonstration with the class.)

When both tasks have been completed, explain to the groups that they are now ready to construct the second page of their book. It will be headed 'Changes in the animal world' with a sentence at the bottom such as 'Metamorphosis – the life cycle of the frog'. Show the children your mock-up of the peep through wheel page and explain how it works. Demonstrate how:

1. The card circle is attached with a paper fastener to the centre of the page.

2. Each stage in the development of a frog is stuck on so that they can be seen when the wheel is turned.

3. The labelling for that stage is placed outside the wheel beside the picture.

See Figure 2 for an example of how the page may look.

These instructions are explained fully on photocopiable page 174 for the children to follow. Tell each group that they are going to

work together to follow the instructions. They must work collaboratively, discuss what they are doing and share out the tasks in order to complete their page.

The children have now created another page for their 'Changes' book.

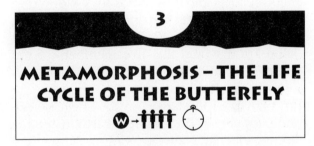

3

METAMORPHOSIS – THE LIFE CYCLE OF THE BUTTERFLY

Teaching content

Changes can be shown by a sequence of pictures and labels. You can follow a pictorial sequence of instructions to make something.

What you need

Selection of reference books (see list on page 158, include some that show the process of metamorphosis, particularly from caterpillar to butterfly), photocopiable pages 175, 173 and 174, A3 cartridge paper, scissors, card (25cm x 25cm), plate (20cm diameter), writing and drawing materials, paper.

What you do

This session is intended to give children further practice of the skills they learned in the previous session. They will construct page 3 of their group books which will be on the life cycle of the butterfly.

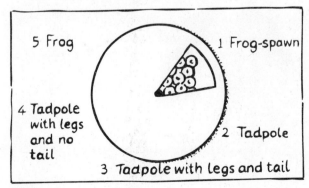

Figure 2

Gather the class together and look at the pages which they created in Session 2. Remind the children of how they created these pages. Five members of the group drew the pictures to show the various stages in the development of a tadpole while the other members constructed the wheel. The whole group then worked together to construct the page. Explain that in this session they will be working through the same process, but that this time they will be creating a page showing the development of a butterfly.

As in the previous session, choose a text book which explains the metamorphic process of the caterpillar and work through the various stages with the children. These being:
• an egg;
• the egg hatches into a caterpillar;
• the caterpillar grows larger;
• it makes a cocoon to protect it while it is changing;
• it emerges as a butterfly.
You may feel it appropriate to read a copy of Eric Carle's book *The Very Hungry Caterpillar* to deepen the children's understanding.

When you feel they have a sufficient understanding of the process, organise the children back into the groups they worked in previously. Give each group leader a copy of photocopiable page 175 and explain that, as before, you would like five members of the group to complete it. (If you wish to make this session more challenging for the children you can blank out the labels on the sheet before photocopying it. The children will then need to discuss with each other the various stages they

have just learned about and write appropriate headings next to each picture. As with page 172 these need only be short.)

Meanwhile the other members of the group will be constructing the peep-through wheel on photocopiable page 173 in the same way as before. When all the groups have finished their various activities, refer them to photocopiable page 174 and explain that they will be using this to create the third page of their book.

CAMOUFLAGE BY CHANGING

Teaching content
You can find information you need from books by using the contents and index pages. Information can be given in pictures and words.

What you need
Selection of reference books (see list on page 158, include some that discuss camouflage in animals), strips of paper and thin card (22cm x 7cm), photocopiable page 176, writing and drawing materials, A3 cartridge paper, adhesive.

What you do
Remind the children of the work they have done so far on metamorphosis – the process which involves some animals changing form dramatically over their life. Explain that in this

session they will be looking at ways in which some animals change their appearance in order to be less noticeable and to blend into their surroundings. Introduce the word 'camouflage' and ask the children if they know what it means. Listen to a few suggestions then ask two children to check the meaning in a dictionary. When you have established with the children what the word means, give them some examples of animals which exhibit camouflage; those whose colourings, patterns and shape help to make them less noticeable. Examples could include tigers, leopards, giraffes, frogs, snakes, lizards, some fish and butterflies.

Explain that some animals have developed their colouring over many thousands of years in order to survive. Other animals are different. They are able to change colour or pattern in order to be camouflaged in new or potentially dangerous surroundings. Ask the children if they can think of what animals these might be. Hopefully they will suggest the chameleon. Ask if they know of any other animal which behaves like this. If they do not, mention the arctic fox and hare, both of which grow different coloured coats in the winter.

Tell the children that they will be working in the same groups as before but this time in pairs. Explain that you would first like each pair to select one animal from those they have discussed, for example the arctic fox. (Each

pair will also need to negotiate with the group as a whole so that they do not all draw the same animal.) Using the thin strips of paper, one child will draw the animal in a summer scene while his or her partner draws the animal in a snowy scene (or which ever surrounding is appropriate for the animal they choose, for instance if they choose the chameleon, a leafy forest and a rocky outcrop). When each pair has drawn their pictures they should return to their group. The children will use their drawings to create the next page of their book. Give each group a copy of photocopiable page 176 which gives instructions and diagrams on how to construct a flap door page. Be on hand to give help and support where necessary.

When the chidren have completed their sheet encourage them to caption their pictures, for example:

> The arctic fox changes colour in snow.
> Or
> The chameleon changes colour to match
> its surroundings.

At the end of this session the children will have completed the next page of their 'Changes' book.

5

CHANGES IN THE PLANT WORLD – GROWTH

Teaching content

You can write a report of a process in writing with pictures to show a sequence over time.

What you need

Photocopiable page 177, broad beans (4 per group), transparent jars, damp cotton wool, blotting paper, selection of reference books (see list on page 158, include some that depict changes in plants and flowers), chalkboard, writing and drawing materials.

What to do

Remind the children that they have been learning about various changes in the world, both changes in people and changes in animals. Explain that in this session the focus will be on changes in plants. Ask the children what they think is the most common type of change in plants. They will probably suggest that plants grow. Explore with the children how plants grow: 'What happens to them? How do they start off?' The children may know that plants start as seeds, they grow shoots and roots and then stems and leaves and possibly flowers. Write these key words – 'seeds', 'shoots', 'roots', 'stems', 'leaves', 'flowers' on the board for the children to refer to. Ask two children to find a book from the selection you have gathered which illustrates this growth process.

Suggest to the children that they could watch and record the growth of a broad bean in the classroom and use the information to create another page for their 'Changes' book.

Distribute a copy of photocopiable page 177. The children set up the jar and beans as shown in picture 1. Each group sets up a jar with damp cotton wool in the base, a piece of blotting paper rolled around the inside and four broad beans placed between the jar and the blotting paper. Explain that two children each week must take responsibility for keeping the blotting paper damp. On the photocopiable sheet the children must add their names to the relevant week, draw a picture of what they see and write a short report beneath their picture such as 'The bean has split open and a shoot and root have sprouted from it'.

When this sheet is completed, give the groups a sheet of A3 paper, explaining that this sheet will form the third page of their 'Changes' book. The children can cut out the individual sections on photocopiable page 177 and paste them on to their A3 cartridge paper, drawing in arrows to show the correct sequence.

6

LEAVES CHANGE COLOUR IN AUTUMN

IconTeaching content

You can give information in pictures, writing and diagrams and test if the pictures are clear.

What you need

Selection of reference books, photocopiable page 178, chalkboard, writing, drawing and painting materials, A4 paper, a selection of autumn leaves (if obtainable), scissors, adhesive, A3 cartridge paper.

What to do

Gather the children together and remind them of the work they have done so far on change. Explain that in this session they will be learning about another type of change in plants – this time in trees. Ask the children to suggest ways in which trees change. The children will probably mention that leaves change colour and eventually fall from the trees. Emphasise the change in leaf colour which take place, that they do not just change from green to brown but undergo other subtle changes in colour. If it is autumn it would be useful to have a selection of leaves of different colours for the children to look at and describe in terms of colours. Ask the children to suggest other

colours and list these on the board – green, brown, greeny brown, bronze, red, orange, russet.

Give each child a copy of photocopiable page 178. Explain that, using this sheet, you would like them to record the changes of colour that occur in leaves in autumn. Give the children paints but tell them they will need to mix the colours to obtain the shades they want. Explain that the first row of leaves on the sheet tells them the colour they need to paint them. The second row has been left blank so that the children can create their own colours and then name them, writing the colours underneath their paintings.

When the children have completed photocopiable page 178, hand out a sheet of A4 paper to each child and tell them to divide the sheet in half horizontally. Model the next part on an A4 sheet for the children to refer to. Draw the outline of two identical trees then fill in one tree as for summer, using appropriate colours, and the other tree as for winter, this time using suitable winter colours. Tell the children that this is what you would like them to do and they can use whichever drawing materials they like.

When the children have finished this part of the session they will each have a completed copy of photocopiable page 178 and a sheet of A4 on which they have drawn their two trees. Each group will therefore have several copies

of both of these sheets. The task for the groups now is to select from these to construct the next page of their book, which can be entitled 'Leaves change colour'.

Organise the children into their groups and give each group a sheet of A3 cartridge paper. Tell them to draw a line across the middle of the sheet and to stick the summer trees on one side and the winter trees on the other. The pictures on either side should not be in any corresponding order. (The page is going to be a puzzle page.) They should number the summer trees 1 to 6 and letter the winter trees A to F. (You may like to include a caption such as 'Can you match the summer tree to its winter partner?'.) The children should take it in turns to try and match the pairs of trees, writing the correct answers on the back of the page. Photocopiable page 178 can be cut up and used to decorate the page.

FEELINGS CHANGE

Teaching content
You can give information in words and pictures. Statements about things, for example feelings, can be justified and explained.

What you need
Selection of reference books (see list on page 158), strips of paper and thin card 22cm x 7cm, writing and drawing materials, adhesive, A3 cartridge paper, photocopiable page 176.

What to do
Gather the children together and tell them that today you are in a good mood. You are feeling very happy because they have been working so hard and have been very well behaved. Ask the children how they can tell you are in a good mood and that you are feeling happy. They may say that they can see from your face – you are smiling, your eyes are bright, your mouth turns up. Emphasise that a person's face can indicate to others their mood or feelings. Make a different kind of face, for instance a worried face, and ask the children what feelings your face shows now. Tell the children about a time you were worried, for example when you thought you had lost your purse or wallet. Ask

them to tell the class of a time when they have been worried and take a few examples. Build up a word bank of mood or feeling words on the board.

Ask the children what other feelings or moods they have experienced. Explore these in a similar way to above and build up a list on the board, arranging them as opposites. These could include:

happy	sad
worried	content
angry	cheerful
comfortable	uncomfortable
embarrassed	relaxed
bored	enthusiastic

Introduce the idea of opposites to the children. For example, 'I know that I'm worried when I'm going to be late but content when I know I have got plenty of time.' 'I'm angry when my children don't come for their tea when I call them but cheerful when they rush in and tell me they are starving and how lovely the tea looks.'

Explore these ideas with examples from the children. When you feel they have a sufficient grasp of the concept, organise them into their groups and tell them that they must choose a mood to write about. (Each child in the group must choose a different mood or feeling.)

Give each child two strips of paper, approximately 22cm × 7cm. On one strip they

should write 'I'm _____ when _____.' For example, 'I'm happy when my friends come to play.' On the second strip of paper they should write 'But I'm _____ when _____.' For example, 'But I'm sad when I'm alone.' They should also illustrate the strips with pictures.

When they have done this, explain that they will be making a flap door page for the next page of their 'Changes' book in the same way that they did for Session 4. Hand out a copy of photocopiable page 176 and set them to work.

When the children have completed their page they may wish to write captions for their strips and glue these on to the page.

ME BEHAVING BETTER

Teaching content
You can give reasons and explanations for the things you do. You can plan to change by making a list of things to try/actions to take.

What you need
Photocopiable page 179 (one per child), A3 sheets of paper (two per group) – one headed 'I behave badly when...' and the other headed 'I'm trying hard to behave better by...', writing materials, scissors, adhesive, A3 cartridge paper.

What to do
Remind the children that in the previous session they talked about moods and feelings. Discuss how what we do and how we behave can affect the moods and feelings of others. Encourage the children to think about things they do which make other people such as their mums, dads, grandparents, teachers, friends feel angry, sad or disappointed. Take a few examples from the children. For instance, one child may say: 'My mum gets angry when I don't do what she asks me.' Another may say 'My brother is sad when I won't play with him'.

Organise the children into their groups and give each group a sheet of paper headed 'I behave badly when...'. Ask them to make a list of the times when they behave badly. For example 'I behave badly when my friend takes my ball; my mum says time for bed; my teacher asks me to do my work again'. Tell the group leader to write down their ideas. Give the children 10 minutes to complete their list.

When the specified time is up, ask each group to show their lists to the class. Explore similarities and differences and establish with the children that we all behave badly sometimes and it is acceptable to feel angry, upset or aggrieved on occasions. Explain that what is important is how we deal with these feelings. 'How can we avoid bad behaviour?' Take some of the children's ideas. For instance they may suggest that a person could take a deep breath when something annoys him or her, must not

hit out without thinking and should consider the situation from someone else's point of view. Give the groups the second sheet of paper headed 'I'm trying hard to behave better by...' and ask them to complete this sheet. The group leader will record their ideas. Give the groups 10 minutes to do this and then bring the groups together again to share their ideas.

Issue a copy of photocopiable page 179 to each child and explain that you would like them to identify times when they behaved badly and then give suggestions as to how they could improve their behaviour. The ideas already brainstormed should help them to make their own action plan on 'Me behaving better'. There are spaces on the sheet for each child to draw two pictures of him or herself.

When each group member has completed her or his sheet the group leader should collate the pages. Explain that the next page of their book will be called 'Changing behaviour'. Issue a sheet of A3 cartridge paper to each

group (or several sheets if necessary) and explain that you would like them to cut out the various sections from their photocopiable sheets to form the next page of their book. The children can design the page by:
1. selecting examples from the sections 'I behave badly when';
2. cutting out their various examples of 'I'm trying hard to behave better by';
3. cutting out their picture of 'The perfect me'. Together the children should choose an arrangement which they feel best displays these various sections and then paste them on to their A3 sheet.

CHANGE – GOOD OR BAD?

Teaching content
Taking notes helps us to remember. We can use notes to build up information and write it down for others. We can discuss the negative and positive effects of change.

What you need
Selection of reference books (see list on page 158, choose some that focus on changes in society), scrap paper, writing and drawing materials, large sheet of newsprint (one per group), marker pens, A4 paper, A3 cartridge paper.

What to do
Talk with the class about all the changes they have been finding out about and working on over the past few sessions. Ask the children whether they think these changes are positive – a good thing, or negative – a bad thing. Work through some examples to stimulate the children into thinking about this. 'Is it a good thing that plants grow and change? Why? Is it good that animals change colour to protect themselves? Why?'

Give each child a piece of scrap paper. Tell the children that you are going to tell them about some changes which they have not yet explored. Select a book or books from the selection you have gathered which discuss changes in society and read these to the children. Tell the children that as you read, you would like them to make notes. In your talk focus on changes, particularly in the last 50 years, and call on your own experiences to focus on:

• changes in fashion, for example in clothes and shoes
• changes in people as they grow older – how they look; what they need
• changes in technology – in the home; in school
• changes in people's lives – shopping; leisure interests.

When you have finished reading, take each of these in turn and explore with the children whether these changes are good or bad. Ask 'Is it a good or bad thing that fashion changes? Is it good or bad that we have trainers now which people didn't have in the 1950s? Is it good or bad that we have more selection of things to buy in our shops?' Encourage the children to give opinions but also to justify them, for example 'I think it's bad to have very expensive trainers because some people don't have enough money to buy them and may feel left out'.

Emphasise that some changes can have both positive and negative effects. For example, many people now have colour televisions and videos. In many ways this could be seen as good because people get a lot of enjoyment from the television, yet the downside could be that television requires no social interaction and so isolates people which means that they may spend less leisure time with other people.

Organise the children into their groups and give each group leader a large sheet of newsprint and a marker pen. Explain that you would like each group to brainstorm a list of changes they like and changes they do not like. The group leader should write these on the sheet of paper

under two separate columns. These changes could be related to:

• People – for example 'when my mum changes from being angry to being happy'; 'when my dad changes from his work clothes to his track suit'; 'when my teacher gets cross about my work'.
• Places – 'I like the school playground when it gets busy in the morning'; 'I don't like the cinema being pulled down to build a road'.
• Weather – 'I like it when the sun shines on the park'; ' I don't like it when it rains all day on a Sunday'.

When they have completed this brainstorm, each child in the group should select one change they like and one they do not like. Distribute a sheet of A4 paper to each child and explain that they should draw a picture and write a few sentences about the changes they have chosen. When the children have completed their sheets give each group a sheet of A3 cartridge paper. (They may need a couple of sheets.) They should work together in their groups to construct the next page of their book. They must discuss with each other different layouts using the pictures and text they have created and come to a mutual decision. The group leader should write a heading such as 'Changes can be good or bad' and then a sentence such as 'Change is natural' to complete the page.

CONTENTS, GLOSSARY AND INDEX

Teaching content

What is a glossary? How to create contents, index and glossary pages.

What you need

All the children's completed pages so far, A4 paper, writing materials, selection of reference books (include some that have an index, contents page and glossary), dictionary, paper.

What to do

Note: This session may be best covered with each group in turn as the children may need quite a lot of support.

Ask the group to bring out their completed pages and to spread them out on the floor or group table. Tell them to discuss with each other the order in which they would like the pages to go. When this is agreed the group leader should number the pages.

Ask the children how people reading their book will be able to find the page or the information they are looking for. Hopefully, the children will mention the need for a contents page and an index. Encourage them to look at the contents page and the index of some of the reference books you have selected. 'What is the difference between them?' Ensure that the key points are covered:

• The information on the index page is in alphabetical order.

• The index page often contains more items than the contents page.

• Items on the index page may give more than one page number.

• Items on the index page use one key word.

Ask the children whether they can suggest what the contents page of the 'Changes' book will contain. They should suggest that the heading on each page will be the contents and the page numbers will correspond. So a contents page:

• lists the titles of chapters, sections or pages;

• gives this information in the same order as it occurs in the book;

• gives the relevant page numbers.

Tell the children that their book will also need a glossary. Look at some examples with the children from the reference books you have gathered and establish that a glossary

contains:

• new or difficult words which appear in alphabetical order;

• an explanation of the meaning of each of these words.

Ask the group to read their completed pages. After they have read each page tell them to note on a sheet of A4 paper any key words which they will need to include in the index, and any words which will require explanation or definition for inclusion in the glossary. Remind the children that any words that appear in the index must be accompanied by the correct page number.

When the children have finished selecting or noting the words for their index and glossary, three tasks can be completed by the children in each group.

Hand out A4 paper and writing materials and set one pair to work creating the contents page. Other children can create the index. Explain that the children must use the information on their planning sheet to put the words in alphabetical order. They can do this by numbering them or by cutting and ordering them. These words must then be copied on to A4 paper in the correct order with the relevant page numbers beside them. The rest of the children can create the glossary. Stress that these words need to be placed in alphabetical order and that each word will also need a definition which the children must find and copy from an information book or dictionary. When they have completed their work, show them how the various sections can be cut out and pasted on to a sheet of A3 cartridge paper.

FRONT AND BACK COVERS

Teaching content

Front covers and back covers of books contain useful information in a standard format.

What you need

Selection of reference books, chalkboard, writing and drawing materials, adhesive, scrap paper, A3 coloured card, A4 paper, completed 'Changes' pages from previous sessions.

What to do

Bring the class together and explain to them that to complete their group books they need to make a front and back cover. Look at the front cover of some of the reference books you have gathered and ask the children what they contain. The children should mention:
- the title of the book;
- a picture;
- the author's name.

List these points on the board.

Select one of the books and examine the picture on the front cover with the children. 'Is it clear from the picture what the book is about? Is the picture bright, interesting and eye-catching?'

Work through the same process as above with back covers and help the children to compile a list of the key features of back covers. These should include:
- a short summary of what the book is about;
- other titles in the series or by the same author;
- author's biographical details (sometimes);
- a picture of the author (sometimes).

Explain that back covers may not necessarily carry all this information but will probably include some.

Give each group some scrap paper and ask them to note down what they would like their front and back covers to contain. Ask them also to jot down what they would like to say about the authors – themselves.

When they have finished, the group should share out the tasks. Give the children some A4 paper and tell them that you would like two children to draw the picture for the front cover. Two other children can write the title for the front cover and the authors' names. Two children

can write a brief summary of what the book is about. All the children can draw a small picture of themselves and write some brief biographical details.

When the children have completed these tasks, tell them to cut out what they have written and drawn and lay it out on the A3 coloured card which you have provided. They should make sure that it all fits before pasting down the various sections.

When the children have completed their front and back covers they can attach them to the pages of their 'Changes' book. Some copies can be donated to the school library. Others can be given to various classes in the school.

IS OUR BOOK USEFUL?

Teaching content

It is important to evaluate the success of your book. This can be done by asking the user questions and recording the responses in a table.

What you need

Photocopiable page 180, writing materials, children's completed 'Changes' books.

What to do

When other classes have had sufficient time to look through the 'Changes' books given to them by your class, suggest to the children that it would be useful to check on how helpful other people have found them.

Give each child a copy of photocopiable page 180 and look over it with the class, ensuring that the everyone can read it. Explain that each group will visit the class that has read their book. Arrange with the classes when would be the best time to visit.

Send each group to the various classes and encourage them to work in pairs with a group of children in each class. One child can ask the questions and the other can record the group's answers.

On returning to the class the children should share their findings first with the rest of their group and then with the class. Encourage the children to be as constructive and positive as possible in the feedback they give.

CHANGES: WHAT CHANGES AND HOW?

In your groups list how these things change.

People change	Plants change
How?	How?

Animals change	The world changes
How?	How?

METAMORPHOSIS – LIFE CYCLE OF THE FROG

	Tadpole with legs and tail
	Tadpole
	Frog
	Tadpole with legs and no tail
	Frog-spawn

TO MAKE A PEEP THROUGH WHEEL

1. Find a round shape (such as a plate) which measures 20cm in diameter.

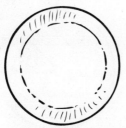

2. Place the shape on to a piece of card bigger than the plate.

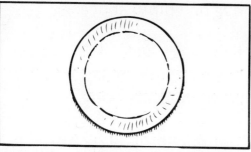

3. Draw round the outside of the plate (the circumference) with a pencil.

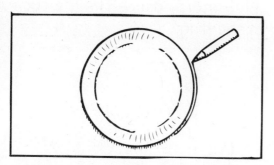

4. Lift the plate off and cut round the pencil mark circle.

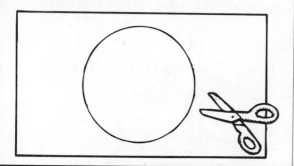

5. Find the centre of the card circle and mark with a pencil.

6. Draw a triangle shape from the centre to near the edge of the circle.

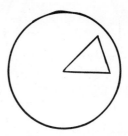

7. Cut out the triangle shape.

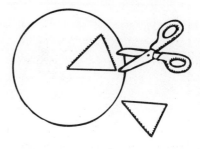

8. You now have a circle of card with a wedge shaped hole in it.

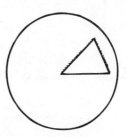

CONSTRUCTING YOUR PAGE

What you need
Peep through wheel, paper fasteners, group pictures and labels, adhesive.

What to do
First pin the peep through wheel into the centre of your A3 cartridge page and secure with the paper fastener.

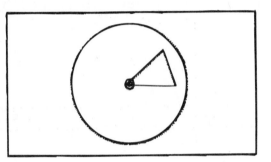

Next select picture 1 (frog-spawn) and stick this picture inside the hole on to the page.

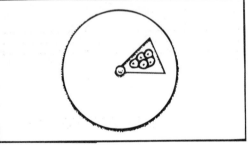

Then glue the label beside this picture.

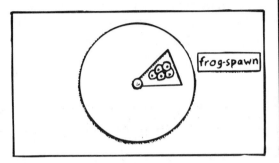

Next turn the wheel to the right (clockwise) until you have an empty space.

Then select picture 2 (tadpole with tail) and stick it into the space on to the page.

Continue until all pictures and labels are complete.
Number the stages 1, 2, 3, 4, 5.
Add the heading 'Metamorphosis – The life cycle of the frog'.

Scholastic
NON-FICTION WRITING PROJECTS
Workshop

LIFE CYCLE OF THE BUTTERFLY

	Egg
	Butterfly
	Small caterpillar
	Fat caterpillar
	Chrysalis

CONSTRUCTING A FLAP DOOR PAGE

What you need
The completed strips of paper, thin card, adhesive, A3 paper.

What you do
Decide how to arrange your drawings on the A3 paper.

| Arctic fox |
| Hare |
| Chameleon |

Stick the 'inside' the door pictures on to the page.

Stick the 'outside' the door pictures on to the thin card.

Paste the left hand side of the card and stick to the pictures as shown.

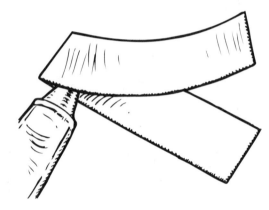

Write captions for your pictures and glue these on to the page.

Scholastic
NON-FICTION WRITING PROJECTS
Workshop

NAME

GROWING A BROAD BEAN

Names				
Date	We set up the jar on	After one week	After two weeks	After three weeks
What we saw				
Written report	We saw	We saw	We saw	We saw

Labels on diagram: jar, broad bean, blotting paper, damp cotton wool

LEAVES CHANGE COLOUR IN AUTUMN

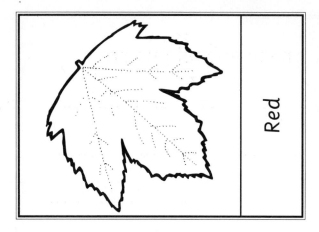
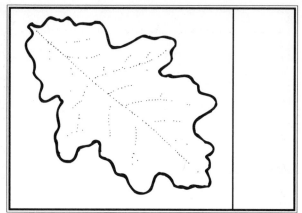

Red

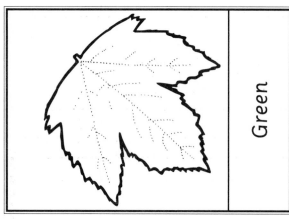
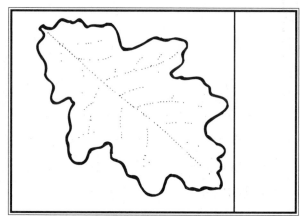

Green

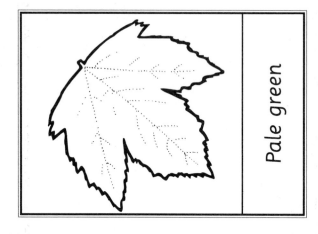
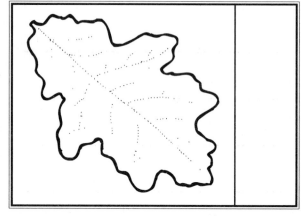

Pale green

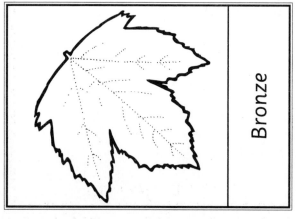
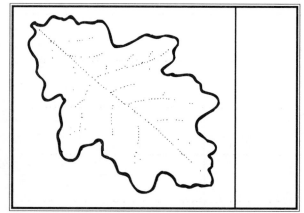

Bronze

Scholastic
NON-FICTION WRITING PROJECTS
Workshop

ME BEHAVING BETTER

I behave badly when

_____

_____

_____

_____

_____

I'm trying hard to behave
better by

_____

_____

_____

_____

_____

_____

_____

The perfect me

IS OUR BOOK USEFUL?

	☺ Yes	☹ No
1. Is it clear from the cover what the book is about?		
2. Is it clear from the cover who wrote the book?		
3. Did the contents page help you to find what you wanted?		
4. Was the information on each page clear and easy to understand?		
5. Were the illustrations interesting?		
6. Did the index page help you to find information?		
7. Did the glossary help to explain words you didn't understand?		
8. Did the back cover give you useful information about the authors?		
What did you especially like about the book?		
What could improve the book?		

Scholastic
WORKSHOP

Chapter Twelve

ME, LOOKING
AFTER MYSELF

INTRODUCTION

Project description

This project has been designed with Year 2 children in mind, although it could be tackled late in Year 1 or early in Year 3. If used intensively, children could complete their booklets in two weeks but a more leisurely approach could result in a three or four week project.

The children first discuss the many different ways in which they can look after themselves, for example by eating healthy foods, keeping clean, taking exercise, getting plenty of rest and sleep, and so on. These topics form the subject of an information book which each child compiles for a relative or special friend. Each section of the book provides opportunities for different ways of presenting information using pictures and words. The first 'chapter' of the book is about 'me', giving individual details such as name, date of birth, family and home. This is followed by chapters on 'Keeping Clean', 'Healthy Eating' 'Taking Exercise', 'Keeping Safe' and 'Resting and Sleeping'. Finally, children are invited to consider others who help to look after them such as mums and dads, and to think about how they can look after others, for instance younger brothers and sisters, friends, and so on. A thank-you letter is written and fixed to the final page of the book. Having completed the information pages of their books children move on to creating a contents page and designing a cover. When the book is completed children discuss the various ways in which it could be presented to the special person of their choice, perhaps at a school presentation, or wrapped up and enclosed with a gift card, and consider how to get feedback from readers.

Why this context?

Not only does this context offer a wide range of functional writing tasks but it gives both the teacher and children an opportunity to discuss a range of issues important for healthy living and relevant to the experience of each child. While each topic could become a project in its own right, the intention is to draw them together under the heading 'Me, Looking After Myself', to give children experience of compiling their own personal booklet.

Project organisation

The focus of this project is on developing each child's individual response to the discussion topics so that he or she can record relevant information in order to create a personal book. While much of the project involves children working individually there is still a need for group and/or class discussion, particularly at the beginning of each session. It is up to individual teachers to decide whether they prefer to develop each session with the entire class or in turn with small groups, whichever best serves the needs of the children.

The project does allow possibilities for differentiation if children are grouped according to skill level. The ways in which children express and record their ideas may be varied. Some children will contribute ideas through discussion and record them in pictorial form. It may be necessary to scribe for these children. Other children will have sufficient skill to write their own text and may prefer to do this before working on illustrations. The teacher will know best what to expect from his or her pupils. In the sessions which follow, ideas are suggested for further development. These can be adapted to provide extension work and ideas for more able pupils.

The project sessions deal only with a small number of issues. Teachers should feel free to extend the study, to change the emphasis, to explore other topics which arise out of discussion or to order the material differently in accordance with the needs, interests and skills of their pupils.

Publication, celebration and review

This topic leads to an identifiable end-product – an information book made by each child. The structure may be shared but the specific contents will vary according to personal experience. From the start children are asked to think about who will receive their book. This means that celebration of publication may take the form of a 'presentation' ceremony or simply that children take their books to the recipients. Self and peer evaluation is built into the final session, as is the idea of getting feedback from readers, either by interviewing them or by asking them to complete a questionnaire.

Books the children may find useful

I Feel Angry by Brian Moses (Wayland, 1994) (Other titles: *I Feel Sad, I Feel Jealous, I Feel Frightened*)
Yourself by Michael Pollard, (Wayland, 1989)

ME, LOOKING AFTER MYSELF

w—† 40

Teaching content

Planning a booklet, deciding what to include (content) and how the chosen content will be sequenced. These decisions are influenced by the intended audience.

What you need

Photocopiable page 193 enlarged to A3 size, photocopiable page 194, writing materials, large sheet of paper, marker pens, highlighter pens, samples of books which have dedications, a blank booklet for each child consisting of three A3 sheets folded in half vertically to create 12 pages – an elastic band should be placed between the crease to act as a spine, see Figure 1. (Alternatively the booklet could be made of at least eight A4 sheets stapled together on the left-hand side.)

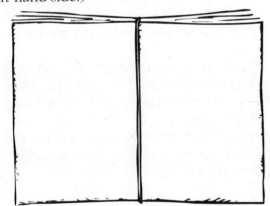

Figure 1

What to do

Note: If preferred project sessions could be carried out as group activities rather than as a whole-class activity.

Gather the class together and show the children your enlarged copy of photocopiable page 193. Ask them to tell you how the child in the poster is looking after herself. Elicit from them the significance of the small illustrations on the sheet. Write the heading 'Me, Looking After Myself' on a large sheet of paper and note the children's suggestions. Try to make sure the following are included:

- eating healthy foods;
- taking exercise;
- getting plenty of rest and sleep;
- saying 'No' to strangers;
- being with friends and family.

Ask the children to think of other ways in which they look after themselves and develop discussion around their ideas. Add further useful suggestions that arise to the list, praising children for their efforts. Point out that as it would be difficult to include so many ideas on a poster, the children could, instead, make an information book with the same title – 'Me, Looking After Myself'.

Introduce the blank booklets you have prepared and show the children that there is plenty of space for information. Explain that everyone will have their own booklet.

Ask the children what they need to think about before starting work on their booklets. They may suggest content: what to write about. If they do, tell them that this is correct but suggest that they first think about their audience: who will read their book? Ask them who they think would be interested in an information book about 'Me, Looking After Myself'. Suggestions are likely to include parents, grandparents, siblings, special friends, and so on. Explain to the children that many books include a dedication and show some examples of these from the selection you have gathered. Tell the children that they must make a personal decision about who will receive their book.

Return to the ideas listed in the first part of the session and ask the children to suggest which ones should be included. Highlight these, then ask the children to suggest how they should be sequenced and why. Discuss the following questions:

- What would be a good starting point? Why?

(Make sure that the first sections explain 'All About Me' and give information or personal details about the author, for example the child's name.)

• What should come next? Why? (Follow the children's ideas but limit the number of items if necessary.)

• How should the books end? Why? (Encourage the children to end on a positive note 'I can help myself and others' or 'I look after my friends and family'.)

Write numbers next to each point so that the children can follow the agreed order. Explain that although they will 'personalise' the contents, everyone can work from the same contents list.

Issue each child with a booklet and a copy of photocopiable page 194. (They may also require a folder in which to store their on-going work.) Explain how the photocopiable sheet is to be completed and allow time for this. The children should first:

• decide on a dedication and write the person's name and why the book is for them;

• make notes from the agreed contents list.

Tell the children that they will work on their booklets in the next session. Before then you would like them to start thinking about their contents plan and collecting material, such as photographs, which might be useful.

Further development

Given more time for thought children may make further suggestions about content. These can be discussed and adopted if appropriate.

Teaching content

Information may be given in words and pictures. The layout of these helps to present the information attractively.

What you need

Booklets from the previous session, photocopiable page 195, writing and drawing materials, paper, adhesive, scissors, photographs if available.

What to do

Gather the children together and tell them that they will be starting work on their 'Me, Looking After Myself' booklets. Ask the children to recall the decisions that were made in the previous session about the contents. Remind them that the first section is to be about – ME!

Tell the children that they should also remember who the book is for – who will be reading it?

Discuss what information should be included on the second page. (Explain that page 1 should be left free for the title and contents.) For example:

• what I look like;

• my name;

• what age I am or my date of birth.

Other information might include:

• where I live;

• my family;

• what I like or dislike;

• what makes me happy/sad.

Ask the children to think about how this information could be recorded. 'What should be written? What should be drawn? Does anyone have photographs they would like to include?'

Give each child a copy of photocopiable page 195 and discuss the various headings. Allow the children time to complete this. The children could also draw a picture of themselves and the other members of their family on a separate sheet of paper. When they have done this, discuss how the information could be transferred to their booklets. Demonstrate how the various sections on the photocopiable sheet can be cut out, arranged and then stuck down. Show that different arrangements are possible. Encourage the children to start work on this, but tell them to explain their arrangement to you before they stick the sections down.

Ensure that 'All About Me' is attached to page 2 of their booklets. The children will be returning to page 1 in a later session to complete the title and contents.

Further development

This page or section can be extended to more than one page if children have more information that they wish to write about.

3
KEEPING CLEAN

Teaching content

An instruction tells you how to do something. Instructions are written in the imperative mood and usually include a sequence of actions, sometimes preceded by a list of items required to carry them out.

What you need

Large sheet of paper, marker pens, writing and drawing materials, paper, scissors, adhesive.

What to do

Gather the children together and explain that the next page of their booklet will be about keeping clean. Discuss with the children why keeping clean is an important part of their project on 'Me, Looking After Myself', and ask them to suggest ideas for a heading or title for this page. For example:

• I look after myself by keeping clean because...
• Keeping clean is important because...
• I keep clean by...

Next move on to discuss possible contents for this page, listing suggestions such as:

• washing face and hands;
• brushing teeth;
• washing hair;
• taking a bath or a shower.

Suggest to the children that one way in which they could show others that they know about keeping clean would be to write or draw a set of instructions. Help the children to talk through instructions for one of the listed items, for example how to wash your face.

Stress that it is important to list *what you need*. In this case it would be a facecloth, soap

and a towel. Next work through the order of *what you do*:

1. Fill the basin with warm water.
2. Wet the facecloth and put soap on it.
3. Rub the soapy cloth over your face.
4. Rinse the cloth in the warm water.
5. Wipe your face with the clean cloth.
6. Dry your face with the towel.

Depending on the children's level of skill their instructions can be recorded in words, as above, or in drawings. Some children may find it easier to organise their thinking first by drawing. If they do prefer to complete drawings, captions can be composed and written afterwards. You may need to scribe for some children.

Tell the children they should also explain why face-washing is important. Ask for some reasons and model a sentence: 'I wash my face because...'.

When you have done this give the children paper and writing and drawing materials. Tell them to give their page the heading that has been agreed. Underneath they should write a subhead such as 'Instructions for...' They should choose one aspect of keeping clean and create an appropriate set of instructions in pictures, words or both. For instance:

• How to take a bath.
• How to brush your teeth.
• How to wash your hair.

Remind the children that they must list what is needed as well as what to do.

When they have finished tell them to cut out what they have written or drawn and paste it on to page 3 of their booklet.

Further development

Some children may wish to extend this section by including more information, such as: their choice of soap, toothpaste, shampoo, bubble bath; an illustration of their bathroom with explanatory captions; a list of rules for keeping clean.

4
HEALTHY EATING
W→✝ (40)

Teaching content

The menu format lists food choices for different meals.

What you need

Empty food packets, food labels and pictures of various foodstuffs, word cards naming each of the different foodstuffs, sample menus, writing and drawing materials, scissors, adhesive, photocopiable pages 196, 197 and 198, selection of reference books on food and nutrition, chalkboard.

What to do

Gather the children together, telling them that the focus of this session will be healthy eating. Introduce the food packets, labels and pictures that you have obtained and ask the children to help you sort them into 'healthy' and 'not so healthy' categories. Make sure that healthy choices include fresh fruit, vegetables, milk, fish and the foods that are high in fibre. Emphasise that foods with high sugar and fat content are not so healthy, nor are those with artificial colours and additives. Introduce the word cards naming the different foodstuffs.

You may also wish to discuss with the children what food does for them. This can briefly be stated as 'makes me go, grow and glow'. Depending on the extent of the knowledge of your class, it may even be possible to discuss proteins, fats, carbohydrates, vitamins and minerals. Some children may mention these words without knowing exactly

what they mean so a discussion could ensue. Have a selection of reference books available for the children to refer to.

Tell them that page four of their booklet will be about looking after myself by eating healthy food, and suggest that they write this section in the form of a menu for breakfast, lunch or dinner. Display word cards for 'menu', 'breakfast', 'lunch' and 'dinner'. Introduce and discuss sample menus.

Give each child a copy of photocopiable pages 196 and 197. Using photocopiable page 196 the children should cut out about three or four appropriate foods for each meal and paste them vertically into the correct columns on photocopiable page 197. So, for example, under the column 'Breakfast' the children may decide to stick a picture of fruit juice, a boiled egg, cereal and a glass of milk. Figure 2 shows an example of a partially completed sheet. You may like to model an example with the children before setting them to work on their individual sheets.

Figure 2

When their menus are completed, tell them that these will be transferred to page 4 of their booklet. Discuss an appropriate heading for this page, such as 'I like to eat healthy foods'.

Further development
Some children might like to carry out further research into healthy eating and produce a page giving suitable recipes for healthy dishes, for instance different kinds of salads. Photocopiable page 198 provides a pro forma sheet on which the children can write or record their recipes.

5
TAKING EXERCISE
W → † 45

Teaching content
Information may be recorded via words and illustrations.

What you need
Large sheet of paper, marker pens, chalkboard, photocopiable pages 199 and 200 photocopied on to thin card, scissors, paper fasteners, an example of a split-pin figure for demonstration with the class.

What to do
Gather the children together, reminding them that the next page of their booklet is to be about taking exercise. Discuss the key questions: 'Why is exercise important? What does it do?' If the children need some ideas you could explain that it:
• helps us to grow strong;
• promotes muscle growth;
• improves the circulation and pulse rate;
• is good for the heart and lungs.

Next ask the children: 'How can we take exercise? What do we enjoy?' Answers are likely to include running, skipping, walking, dancing, playing football, tennis, rounders, gymnastics, judo, and so on.

Create a wordbank of action words by noting on a large sheet of paper the children's key words and ideas such as 'run', 'hop', 'jump', 'balance', 'stretch', 'leap', 'skip'.

Next discuss with the children how they could present this information in their personal books. Suggest that they could make a moveable

figure. Show the children the split-pin figure you have created and demonstrate how its limbs can be moved to any position. Give each child a copy of photocopiable pages 199 and 200 that you have photocopied on to thin card and explain that they should cut out the different limbs and attach them together using paper fasteners. The black dot on each limb indicates where an incision should be made and the paper fastener inserted. (Due to the amount of cutting and fastening in this session you may find it helpful to enlist the support of a classroom assistant who can provide extra support to the children.)

When the children have completed their figure, show them how to attach it to page 5 of their booklet. (An extra black dot has been provided at the top of the head so it can be fixed to the page.) Write the starter sentence 'Taking exercise is good for me because...' on the board and ask the chidren to copy it into their book and complete it. When they have done this tell them they can write appropriate action words and sports that they like around the figure. The children can refer to the wordbank created earlier in the session if they need ideas, for example 'run', 'hop', 'gymnastics', and so on

Further development
Some children might like to create a series of action drawings of themselves taking part in sport or exercise, or provide photographs.

KEEPING SAFE

Teaching content
A mini-poster sends a strong message with pictures and words.

What you need
Large sheet of paper, marker pens, enlarged copy of photocopiable page 193 from Session 1, photocopiable page 201, writing and drawing materials.

What to do
Gather the children together and discuss how they will tackle the 'Keeping Safe' page of their booklets. Refer back to your enlarged copy of photocopiable page 193 and look again at how it tackles 'stranger danger'. Encourage the children to talk about other dangers they are aware of and ways in which they can keep safe. For example:
• railway lines – Do not cross the tracks!
• road traffic – Follow the Green Cross Code!
• ponds and canals – Stay on the banks!
• power lines – Do not climb on pylons!
• fire – Do not play with matches!
Note the children's ideas on a large sheet of paper.

Suggest to the children that they design a mini-poster for page 6 of their booklet. They should do this in pairs, choosing one of the

dangers that have been listed and creating a poster designed to raise people's awareness of that danger and help them to keep safe. Give each pair a copy of photocopiable page 201 and explain that they can use this to draft their ideas. Later each child can work independently to transfer their ideas to their individual booklets. Provide a variety of materials and techniques, such as paper, card, paint, and photographs for this stage.

Further development
Some children may wish to add more poster pages to their books showing their awareness of different dangers and indicating how they intend to keep themselves and others safe.

Particularly effective mini-posters might be enlarged for display in school corridors.

RESTING AND SLEEPING

Teaching content
Pictures with captions can be used to convey information.

What you need
Large sheet of paper, marker pens, photocopiable page 202, scissors, adhesive, drawing materials, clothes or fabric catalogues.

What to do
Gather the children together and discuss page 7 of their booklet. Explain that this page will be about the importance of getting plenty of rest and sleep. Ask the children to think about why rest and sleep are important and note their ideas on a large sheet of paper.

Give each child a copy of photocopiable page 202 and explain that the sheet contains a starter sentence for them to complete, a picture of a bed, a figure and two clock faces. Tell the children that they need to complete these items in order to create a self-portrait of themselves in bed. They should first of all decorate the duvet cover on the bed. They could either draw a cover or cut out a pattern from the catalogues and paste it on. They should then draw a face and some night clothes on the figure on the photocopiable sheet. The children should then cut out the figure and cut across the slot on the

Scholastic
NON-FICTION WRITING PROJECTS
Workshop

bed. The figure can then be 'put to bed'. When they have done this the children should complete the clock faces with their bedtimes and getting up times. Finally they should complete the sentence at the top of the sheet 'I need rest and sleep because...'. All these items should then be cut out and pasted into the individual booklets. (This can be done 'step by step' as a directed activity, but if children are to work independently it may be necessary to model what is required by showing the various stages and a completed example.)

Children may discuss adding further details, such as teddy bears, hot water bottles and bedside tables. A dream bubble and/or a speech balloon could also be added to the completed page if they wish.

Further development

Some children might enjoy writing a sense poem about being in bed. For example:

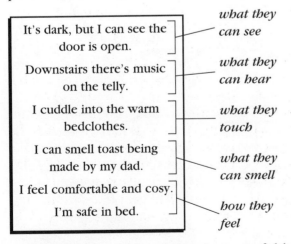

It's dark, but I can see the door is open.	*what they can see*
Downstairs there's music on the telly.	*what they can hear*
I cuddle into the warm bedclothes.	*what they touch*
I can smell toast being made by my dad.	*what they can smell*
I feel comfortable and cosy. I'm safe in bed.	*how they feel*

The poem could be written, cut out, folded if necessary and fixed to the next page in their booklet.

8

RELATIONSHIPS – FAMILY AND FRIENDS

Ⓦ→🧍 ㊿

Teaching content

A letter is one way of telling someone what you are thinking.

What you need

Large sheets of paper, marker pens, photocopiable pages 203 and 204, writing and drawing materials, scissors, adhesive.

What to do

Gather the children together and tell them that the final page of their booklet is to be about other people – people who help to look after them, such as their mums and dads, grandparents, aunts, uncles and neighbours, and people that we can help to look after, for instance, younger brothers and sisters and friends. Take some time to discuss these ideas, allowing children to give examples of people and how they help or are helped. List them on a large sheet of paper. For example:

> **People who help to look after me.**
> My mum helps to look after me by giving me my tea.
> My uncle helps to look after me by taking me to football matches.
> **I can look after these people.**
> I can help my little brother to ride his tricycle.
> I can invite my friends to my birthday party.

Give each child a copy of photocopiable page 203, explaining that they can complete this using words and/or pictures. When they have completed the photocopiable sheet, children should discuss how the finished work can be cut out and pasted to page 8 of their booklets.

When they have completed this part of the session, ask the children whether they would like to write a thank-you letter to someone in their family thanking them for looking after them. Photocopiable page 204 allows the children to write or draw a thank-you letter to someone, perhaps the person to whom their book is dedicated.

Give the children time to think about who they will write to, before asking them to think about what they want to say.

Discuss how to begin the letter. Remind them to write their own address and the date in the top right-hand corner. Ask for ideas about what to say and note useful words and phrases on a large sheet of paper for the children to refer to. Also note ideas about how the letter could be finished. Children may select from these and/or use ideas of their own.

Show children where to write or draw on the photocopiable sheet, explaining that the finished letters should be cut out and folded then placed in an envelope which can be attached to page 8 of their booklets.

Further development
Children might like to bring in photographs of important family members and friends to include on this page. They should write captions for each photograph.

Some children may wish to rewrite their letters and send them to the people concerned.

MAKING THE BOOK: CONTENTS PAGE
9

W→♟ 40

Teaching content
A contents page helps readers to locate different sections of a book. Page numbers also assist the reader in this process.

What you need
Samples of information books which have contents pages, large sheet of paper, marker pens, photocopiable page 205 (plus an enlarged copy for demonstration with the class), scissors, adhesive, writing and drawing materials.

What to do
Gather the children together, telling them that now they have written about all the agreed topics it is time to finish their book. Remind them that they have made an 'information' book and ask them to think about what their book still requires. Tell each group to examine one of the information books, then take feedback, listing their points on a large sheet of paper. Hopefully, the children will suggest that

pages should be numbered, a cover designed, and a contents list created. Explain that the cover design will need some preparation time. Children should start thinking about it now so as to be able to gather any special materials, such as photographs, before the next session.

Tell the children that in this session they will tackle the page numbers and contents list. Ensure that the children understand why these are needed by asking them to give reasons for their inclusion. Note their ideas. For instance, they help you to find the parts of the book you want to read.

Refer the children again to the information books and ask them to look at where the page numbers are placed. Discuss the best placing for numbers – at the top of the page, at the bottom, in the corner? Decide which to use and let the children number the pages of their books.

Give each child a copy of photocopiable page 205 and explain that it lists all the sections they have written about for their booklet. The children's task is to cut out the section headings and stick them on to the contents page in the correct order, then add the appropriate page numbers for each section. (This may vary if some children have added extra pages in some sections. Some blank sections are given in case you have adapted the project with your class.) Use an enlarged version of photocopiable page 205 to model how to build up the contents

page layout on a large sheet of paper. Set the children to work on this task, explaining that they can add a decorative border if they have time.

Further development

Year 3 children could also make an index and glossary for their books. If you have a copy of the *Non-fiction Writing Skills (Key Stage 1)* book you may like to refer to the activity 'What is a Glossary?'.

10

MAKING THE BOOK: COVER DESIGN
Ⓦ→✝ ㊵

Teaching content

The cover of an information book should reflect its contents, as well as giving details of the title and author.

What you need

Samples of information books with a range of styles in cover design, different-coloured A3 or A4 card or paper for covers, marker pens, scissors, adhesive, large sheet of paper, writing and drawing materials, photocopiable page 206.

What to do

Gather the children together and discuss designing the cover for their books. Show them some books, asking them to pay particular attention to the cover design. Tell them to look at the words. What information is given in the title? What kind of lettering is used? Colour? Size? Then tell them to look at the pictures. What information is given there? Have photographs been used or has the picture been drawn? Finally, discuss the layout. Does it have borders? Frames? Different colours?

Discuss with the children what the cover artwork does. Explain that it often informs the reader about the content of the book. What do the words on the front cover do? They inform the reader of the book's title and author. Why is layout important? It makes the book look attractive and interesting and encourages the reader to look inside.

Ask the children to think about designing the covers for their own books. What words and pictures should be used? What size of lettering would be appropriate? Which colours would stand out?

Show the children the range of paper and card which you have prepared. Ask them to review the contents of their books and to consider whether some drawings might be repeated on the cover. If photographs are available, ask the children to think about how they will be used.

Give each child a copy of photocopiable page 206, explaining that this will allow them to plan their own cover design. When they have completed the sheet, ask them to show it to you before allowing them to complete a final copy of the cover on card or cartridge paper.

When the covers have been completed the pages can be inserted. Depending on what is available in your school you may be able to laminate the covers, add spiral binders, and so on. If children have taken time and trouble to create a worthwhile book it is important to provide an appropriate means of finishing their work.

Further development

Some children may point out that the back cover of a book also carries information. Sometimes this gives information about the contents or about the author. This could be an optional extra activity for those children who wish to do more.

It's possible that children will also mention the publisher. This gives you an opportunity to talk about the role of publishing companies and the work that they do. If children in different classes are making books the school could act as publisher and a name could be agreed.

PRESENTATION

Teaching content
Reviewing what has been created is an important part of the work process which includes self-evaluation, but the success or effectiveness of a book really depends on the reader's or audience's response.

What you need
Large sheet of paper, marker pens, the finished book made by each child, photocopiable pages 207 and 208, writing materials.

What to do
Gather the children together and review the finished books. Discuss how they will be given to the dedicatees and plan how to get feedback from the readers.

First allow the children time to show their books to each other and to praise each other's efforts. Ask each child to identify a page or section which they feel they have done particularly well and to talk about it.

Remind the children that the books have been made to give to a special person. Ask the children to state who their books are for – mum, gran, uncle John. Ask the children to think about how their book could be given to that person. For example it could be:
• taken home and handed over;
• wrapped up and enclosed with a gift card;
• sent by parcel post;
• given as part of a presentation to the person at school.

Discuss with the class what should be done. You may decide to keep the presentation very simple or to turn it into a special event.

Suggest to the children that it would be good to know what other people liked about their books, and discuss how this could be achieved. Possibilities include:
• getting children to interview the recipients and note their replies. Show the children a copy of photocopiable page 207 and model some questions that the children could ask. Children can then be given their own individual copies of photocopiable page 207 and transfer the questions, or think of some others, on to their sheets.
• asking the recipients to send back a response slip (photocopiable page 208 provides a list of questions for the recipient to answer).
The children will suggest other ideas.

Ask the children to decide which task to undertake and discuss how they will complete it. Note that time will be required later to discuss the feedback from readers.

Further development
As a result of the feedback some children may like to develop new ideas or to make another book. However, this session should bring the project to a satisfying close.

ME KEEPING HAPPY, SAFE AND HEALTHY

Exercise

Rest and sleep

Stranger danger

Say No!

Friends/
Relationships

My family

Food

LOOKING AFTER MYSELF

This book is for _____

because _____

_____

I shall write about

1.

2.

3.

4.

I shall need drawings or photographs of

HERE I AM

My name is _____

I am ____ years old. My birthday is on _____

This is where I live

My address is

I feel happy when I _____

I feel sad when I _____

I like _____

I do not like _____

MAKE A MENU

cereal   salad   pizza   fish

baked potato   fried egg   fruit juice   trifle

vegetables   pasta   porridge   chicken

burger   milk   banana   lasagne

lentil soup   chips   boiled egg   hot drink

Scholastic
NON-FICTION WRITING PROJECTS
Workshop

HEALTHY EATING

I eat healthy foods because _____

_____

Choose some healthy foods for		
Breakfast	Lunch	Dinner

A RECIPE FOR HEALTHY EATING

What you need

What you do

EXERCISE (1)

Cut out the shapes to make a figure.

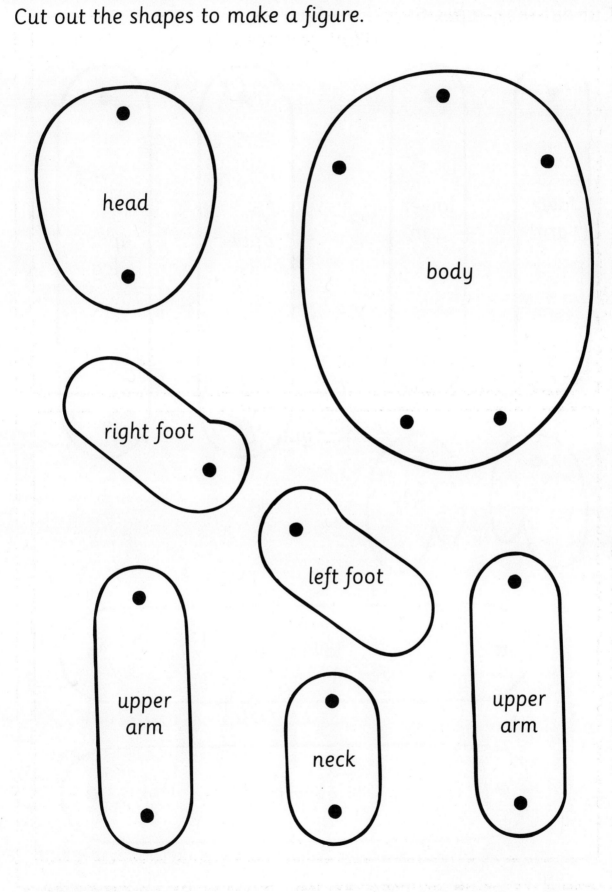

EXERCISE (2)

Cut out the shapes to make a figure.

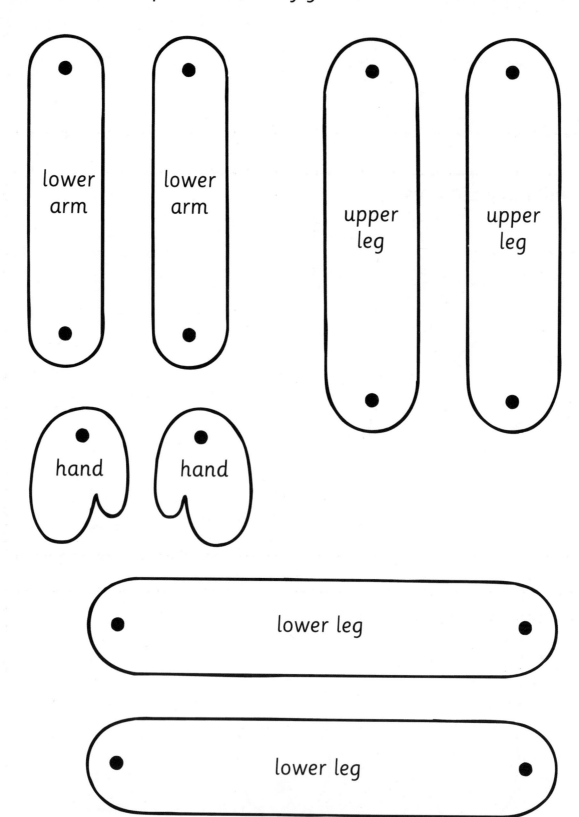

Scholastic
NON-FICTION WRITING PROJECTS
Workshop

KEEPING SAFE

Our poster is about

It will have pictures of

On the poster we will say

REST AND SLEEP

I need rest and sleep because _____

_____

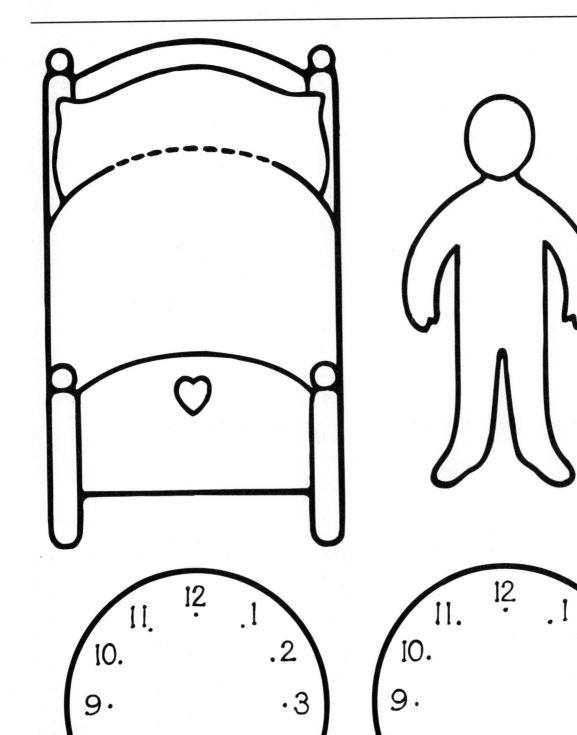

LOOKING AFTER EACH OTHER

These are some people who look after me:

This is what they do:

These are people I look after:

This is what I do:

THANK YOU!

In the box you can write a thank-you letter to somebody who helps to look after you.

Write your own address and the date.

_____

_____

_____

_____

_____

Dear _____

Thank you

With love from

CONTENTS PAGE

All About Me	*page*
Family and Friends	*page*
Healthy Eating	*page*
Keeping Clean	*page*
Keeping Safe	*page*
Rest and Sleep	*page*
Taking Exercise	*page*
	page
	page

PLANNING THE COVER

The book title is

The author is

The cover will look like this.

Scholastic
NON-FICTION WRITING PROJECTS
Workshop